Sacred Earth

Torrey James Lystra

Sacred Earth
Published in 2018 by Red Hawk Books
Copyright c 2018 by Torrey James Lystra
All rights reserved
Printed in USA

Contact torreylystra@gmail.com

Special thanks to Catherine TerBurgh and Carol Lystra for their editing assistance

Cover painting by Torrey James Lystra entitled "Sacred Earth"

The Library of Congress has catalogued this edition as follows:
Library of Congress Control Number: 2018935611
Red Hawk Books, Gig Harbor, WA
Lystra, Torrey James, 1952
"Sacred Earth"
ISBN 0989285170
ISBN 13 9780989285179
PBK.

TABLE OF CONTENTS

INTRODUCTION

"Sacred Earth" is the fourth and final book in this angel directed series of writing. This volume addresses topics such as human origin, human destiny, soul immortality, seven things you need to know, Earth axis realignment, crop circles, purification, megalithic stones, our true beginnings, reincarnation, healers and seers, cosmic consciousness, Shamballa, Atlantis, Lemuria, and so much more.

The information revealed within is organized for easy access to review or ponder that which you have an interest. These 88 questions and answers were born from the mystical, meditative, and spiritual wisdom I came into this life with after numerous lifetimes. They were also influenced by my walk as a healer and seer over the last 28 years as described and revisited "In the Spirit of Black Elk: Preserving a Sacred Way", "An Angel and a Shaman", and "88 Keys to Unlocking the Enlightened Soul". These true stories describe this lifetime after the restoration of sight to a blind eye in one of my sons during a Native ceremony, an initiation ceremony within the Great Pyramid where I first encountered a very real angel, and moments from healing and teaching rituals in which important knowledge was shared.

Mystery, sweat, intent, fate, karma, past lives, soul, focus, study, practice, commitment, curiosity, natural law, courage, prayer, fasting, love, and more, may be found within "Sacred Earth". Before you begin your journey within this new volume, I would like to again pass along to you some advice given to me by the celestial being referred to above. These were her words to me that I hope you may also find useful.

"In order for you to be happy you must first consciously choose the outcome of happiness above all the other choices that will be available to you while you occupy the body you currently reside in. Try to be compassionate and caring towards others. Kindness is a proper response to almost every action while you are on Earth. Try to be in service to humanity in some manner. Not only will you be a positive influence on the society you are a part of, but those in service to mankind are usually moving towards the activation of the supernatural talents that exist potentially within every human soul. If you acquire important knowledge or wisdom on your journey, please share it without your primary concern being financial compensation. This refreshing attitude will still be rewarded in an appropriate manner, and you may avoid a pathway related to greed and avarice which is wrought with peril. Rejoice and be grateful for your life. To live a life filled with joy allows you to walk in gratitude for all the blessings you have received and it is with gratitude that you are able to communicate with Great Spirit in a direct manner. Express what you love, not what you hate. Haters are usually shallow, selfish, angry, and violent beings, while those who know and express love possess the highest most wondrous aspect of being human. Respect all beings, not just the human variety. Some people are too arrogant to respect all life and fall short of the highest benefits of this worthy virtue. Do not get too high or too low with your successes or failures, as they are simply experiences you have chosen to learn from. Take care of your body as you may need it to accomplish all that you came here for. If you occupy a body that is in ill health, try to learn from that experience that you more than likely chose for yourself either between lives or unknowingly via the universal law of cause and effect in this cycle of living. Be willing to acknowledge new ideas and opinions. Do not hurry through your life, savor it like fine wine and be free."

May the words that I share be like a gentle wind moving sweetly through your immortal soul.

DEDICATION

This writing is dedicated to my beautiful and talented wife. We have been happily married now for over 40 years and she continues to be one of the most unselfish, caring, ethical human beings I have ever known. She is also my best friend. We first met as freshmen during our years at the University of California at Santa Barbara and almost immediately began sharing our memories from our past lifetimes together. Direct proof of those past lives made our walk together quite magical from the very beginning. We have been blessed with four sons, their wonderful wives, nine grandchildren, and many wonderful friends.

Our adult lives took shape in park settings while I was employed as a park ranger and supervising park ranger in the San Diego County region of California. We eventually moved to Washington State where we found the tall trees, clean air, and flowing waters of the North Country my angel described to me in the Great Pyramid. Carol has served our community as a Labor and Delivery Nurse at several local hospitals sharing her talents to help bring thousands of babies into the world and continues to thrive as a fantastic Grandmother for our own growing clan.

SACRED PIPE PRAYER

The words I have utilized at my own Sacred Pipe ceremonies come to mind now as you begin this reading.

"Draw a breath of smoke from this Sacred Pipe. Do so as a breath of gratitude to Great Spirit for your life and all that you have become. Utilize the smoke to represent your thoughts and aspirations as you focus on creating what you have prayed for. Let your thoughts be filled with love towards the Earth and each being that lives with you here.

May you realize that every breath you take in life is sacred."

May you gain the knowledge you need through the words you are about to read...

QUESTION 1

Q Could you please explain your view that we are immortal and will each reach perfection in a future age?

TJL Each human body you take on through the process of reincarnation has limits. It is born and it will die. However, what you really are is a soul. As your soul grows and matures over many lifetimes the real "I" that is you will be preserved in that metaphysical vehicle forever. Your highest aspects will be preserved and accompany your movements into new bodies each life you lead. My angel states that this version of humanity will reach perfection by the seventh world of the seventh renewal of our planet Earth many years into the future. Some of you may reach that pinnacle before that point in time.

QUESTION 2

Q You mentioned in our ceremony tonight the seven things that make up every human being and how you felt knowledge about each of those parts could help us as we go about our lives. Would you review that information with us now?

TJL Those seven things define us as human beings. They are not levels of a human being but are what make each of us human:

The first of these things is our physical body. This is the least important of these seven aspects of humankind and yet we must each master the care and attention of our bodies since they house the living Spirit that resides within us.

The second of these things is our astral body. This body appears similar to our physical body yet is composed of a finer matter that remains invisibly connected to our physical body by a thread of light to its ethereal form on the astral plane.

The third of these things is our vital force which many others refer to as prana. This is universal energy and essential to our lives. It is found in all things having life, in every atom, and is everywhere. We utilize it in its material manifestation yet it is not matter.

The next four things go to make up the thinking part of a human being and are considered higher than the first three. They function on three separate planes that at times blend imperceptibly with each other as we advance in the unfoldment of our soul. They comprise our intelligence.

The fourth of these things is our instinctive or animal mind. The instinctive mind is responsible for passions, desires, instincts, and brute emotions. We will discard this aspect of mind at the moment of our death along with the previously mentioned three.

The fifth thing, and the first of the next three aspects of mind that are infinite and become a permanent part of our soul, lifetime after lifetime, is self-consciousness or intellect. This aspect of mind allows us to sense our first conception of the "I" that is who we really are, and we begin to think for ourselves, analyze, and draw conclusions.

The sixth thing is our spiritual mind. This aspect of mind directly aids us in the growth and maturity of our soul and is where inspiration and all that we consider good, noble, and great reside.

The seventh thing is Spirit. I call this our Divine Spark. Masters refer to this aspect as the soul within the soul and words do not really do it justice. It is that something within us that I call the sacred flame of Great Spirit.

QUESTION 3

Q I have heard you mention a "Sacred Way" on numerous occasions and I wonder if you would briefly explain what that is?

TJL At the center of the "Sacred Way" I have described is the path of the sun, moon, planets, and stars. I hold a reverence for the passing of the four seasons within my "Sacred Way". I realize that all natural things in this universe have their own "Sacred Way" of sharing a balance with each other. My "Sacred Way" is not just about one person moving in only one direction. It includes all our lives in a spiral without end as we all move towards enlightenment. Each being acts as a mirror to form our world and each human being is a potential holder of the central flame of pure divinity. Having experienced this sublime reality I am able to at times mirror the strength of Nature lit by my soul which contains the wisdom of Great Spirit. In that inner sanctuary the subtle essence and power of this "Sacred Way" can be found. The pathway to enlightenment is found within each of you.

QUESTION 4

Q After attending your stone-people-lodge ceremony this evening I am enamored with the clarity
I feel. It seems that purification is an important
component to the "Sacred Way" you have shared
with us. Would you care to comment on this feeling that now fills me up?

TJL Purification is a simple concept in which
cleansing the body provides a person with a pure
receptacle for Divine principle to manifest within.
A contaminated receptacle may lead to confusion,

illness, or actions that are not of the highest consciousness. Kindness, compassion, and unselfishness, are outward signs of the pure heart and mind of the enlightened shaman. A shaman in this state is able to communicate with the intelligence of Great Spirit through different elements within Nature. We are able to discern the difference between malevolent energies and benevolent energies in all dimensions. We are able to literally construct our lives to be free to go where Spirit leads us. We have the ability to leave our physical bodies behind to explore other realms when that is called for in ceremony. We are able to listen to our spirit guides from other planes to understand how best to serve others with our work. We are able to at times manipulate space and time.

QUESTION 5

Q I am curious what your thoughts might be regarding the megalithic stones that exist in many locations over the surface of our planet?

TJL Due to the relationship I have with stones, I naturally have been intrigued by the megalithic stones found in many settings and patterns on the Earth. These stones are usually too enormous to understand how they were put in their present locations. On a recent trip my wife and I took to England, Scotland, and Wales that fascination was further enhanced. I believe stones found at places such as Stonehenge, Woodhenge, and Superhenge are remnants of ancient powerful ceremonial environments related to animated stones in which phenomena beyond our present understanding was manifested via there careful placement and relationship to certain constellations and planets. Spiral designs found on many of the singular megalithic stones scattered throughout those regions brought for me stone memories having to do with dimensional travel in a distant age. Other spiral designs seemed to be direct references to the eternal aspect of every human soul perhaps left as reminders to eventually help us with the evolution of our souls in this age.

QUESTION 6

Q Would you speak to us about the action of vision quest your Grandfather Black Elk and Red Buffalo shared with you over their years of teaching?

TJL   "In the Spirit of Black Elk: Preserving a Sacred Way" and in "an Angel and a Shaman" I share specific instructions about this topic, so please refer to that writing for individual stories I shared about my experiences and their teaching. I am happy, however, to give you an overview of the importance of vision quest and what exactly it is.

A hanbleycha is the Lakota word and form of questing for a vision in which the participant goes up on a mountain to pray, meditate, sing, dance, and seek direct contact from Great Spirit or his spirit helpers. Hanbleycha's are usually completed with a sacred pipe, prayer ties, spirit robes, sage, sweet grass, drum, medicine bag, star blanket, any other articles of power that an individual deems important. It is traditional to complete a stone-people-lodge both before and after what was often up to four days and nights of a hanbleycha with a humble shaman overseeing the process. The vision quester is brought up on the mountain and is taken down when the appropriate time arises by the attending shaman. No food or water is consumed on these traditional sacred journeys.

Other forms of vision quests have been completed in many less structured modified ways throughout time by many societies. Grandfather used to tell me that no matter how much physical time is spent in solitude within Nature it is usually a special action and often rewarded by a direct connection to Spirit in some manner. My own spirit helpers required I carry out my hanbleycha's on my own, with no human interpreter acting as an intermediary giving their opinion about what had taken place. They believed I needed to work with the higher powers in a direct manner on my own to seek those answers. My spirit guides divided what was usually 48 hours or more into four segments of 12 hours each which Grandfather referred to as my days on the hill. They expected me to have the strength to make it up and down the mountain myself and remain aware enough to return safely. No food or water was ever consumed during my sacred time "on the hill". As I shared in my writing I found my hanbleycha's to be always extremely important in acquiring the levels of powers required to carry out my work as a humble shaman.

I am also a proponent of any variation of the above if you are able to set aside sacred time with Great Spirit. Know your body and gage your own health so your practice can be both powerful, successful, and safe. Even a few hours spent in the silence communing with Great Spirit may be life changing. Please understand that my "Sacred Way" has evolved over my 28 years on this walk due to the sound advice and guidance of my angel and my other spirit helpers. All humble shamans walk in their own unique ways due to the advice of their spiritual allies.

QUESTION 7

Q Are there such things as magical words?

TJL To pronounce a word is to evoke a thought, and as you know I have always taught you there is great power in a thought. Thoughts are actually things with mass. Because they have mass they exert gravity. Gravity pulls things towards it. If many people focus on the same thought as in a group prayer then the gravitational force of that thought becomes tangible and can have a measurable effect on out physical world. There are also hidden influences attached by supreme wisdom to certain elements within certain words, therefore words indeed have the potential to hold innate power though unknown to most people. Also frequency and vibration can play a role in the power of words as exhibited in the ancient ceremonial songs utilized in a stone-people-lodge some of which were gifts from spiritual allies. The words Jesus spoke at the time he brought several people back to life were words of the highest power from the supreme wisdom I referenced.

QUESTION 8

Q Could you help me understand what you referred to as "supernatural talent" or "spiritual gift" you have experienced in your work as a humble shaman? Also, what is the difference between a humble shaman's perception and that of the average man?

TJL Unlike the average man, a humble shaman has a deep respect for that which transcends human understanding. We have learned never to close our minds to an idea or event simply because it seems miraculous. A humble shaman of the highest power also understands that being alive is an extraordinary journey and we are grateful for each moment. We are able to see that our world and those other worlds that we are linked with are connected by Great Spirit. What Grandfather Black Elk referred to as "supernatural talent" or "spiritual gift" to bring about what others might refer to as miracles, from my angel's words exists in an innate potential state within the soul of every human being that is dedicated to helping other beings. Calling these spiritual powers "super natural" is simply a way to identify them as beyond what many would consider as normal in mainstream thought. Virtually every mystical tradition on Earth is aware that there exists arcane knowledge stored within a soul that is capable of imbuing human beings with these powers. The secret hides within is the core tenant of the ancient mysteries, urging mankind to seek God not in the heavens, but within ourselves. "The kingdom of God is within you", was taught by Jesus the Christ. "Know thyself", was taught by Pythagorus. "Know ye that ye are gods", was taught by Hermes. Historically the power of our human souls has remained hidden, has been misrepresented, mistranslated, manipulated, and thought to be myth. The avatar Jesus knew this power to be very real when he stated, "As I do you can do also".

"Supernatural talent" or "spiritual gift" also includes:

* certain knowledge about the eternal aspects of the soul of man,
* the ability to read the mind of any being in any universe,
* the awareness of all past lifetimes,
* the ability of assuming any form in any universe,
* the ability to understand any sound in any universe.

*   the insight into the nature of any object in
    any universe.

Only a being who achieves perfect enlightenment
will acquire them all.

QUESTION 9

Q Could you please explain to me what a sacred pipe is and how it is utilized to help others?

TJL A "Sacred Pipe", or Chanunpa in the Lakota language, is a ritual implement primarily utilized by sacred men and women in their healing work. It usually consists of an elbow or L-shaped stone bowl connected to a wooden stem. The stone bowl is filled with a smoking mixture of simple herbs and natural tobacco. It is smoked reverently to communicate with "Spirit" and to consecrate most actions of the "Sacred Way" that I have described.

Grandfather Wallace Black Elk considered it "the most sacred implement in the world".

The bowl of a typical Sacred Pipe is most often made of a red stone called catlinite. It represents the Earth and feminine energies. Some Sacred Pipe bowls are intricately carved into forms from the animal nations. The bowl Grandfather and Red Buffalo gifted me is plain with a smooth surface, except where six feather-like dimples are seen around where its stem connects, representing the six directions and powers of our universe. The stem of most Sacred Pipes is made of ash wood smoothed and oiled with animal fat or bees wax. The stem of the pipe Grandfather and Red Buffalo gifted me represents life, and a stem is said to represent male energies. The feather that hangs from my pipe where the stem fits into the bowl is an eagle plume given to me by one of Grandfather's relatives at Wounded Knee. The black shapes within the white of that plume represent the four buffalo that came to me on my vision quest on Bear Butte. It also represents the eagle and all the winged nations. All the beings on this planet and all things in this universe are joined to me when I have filled my pipe asking for help from the West, the thunder beings, from the North, the buffalo nations, from the East, the deer and elk nations, from the South, all other nations, from above, father sky, and from below, earth mother. Everything in the universe is represented by the grains of my smoking mixture. Like a laser, I become focused, I am at the heart of all things and an angel resides in each of the directions within my altar. We are each a part of the whole and the feeling of separation that many people suffer from is an illusion.

In some circles, there are people that believe the Sacred Pipe's powerful attributes should be kept secret. I do not adhere to this line of thought. I believe it should be utilized to help other beings in any way possible. In other circles, people remain skeptical regarding how a stick and a stone can carry any power at all. Wallace Black Elk's adopted Grandfather, Nicholas Black Elk, received his instructions regarding the handling of a Sacred Pipe from a very powerful humble shaman named Elk Head. When we talk about communication with "Spirit" through our Chanunpa's, we are referring specifically to the intelligence of Great Spirit found in all natural things in the universe, whose voice we listen for. When I pull out my Chanunpa from my pipe bag, I purify it each time by smudging it with either sage or sweet grass. Then I utilize an honoring song before I put that stem and that stone together, displaying my eagle plume where they fit together. Sometimes I sit and others times I stand with my feet firmly planted on the earth mother. I invite the powers of the directions to hear my prayers, and ask humbly for their help with each pinch of my smoking mixture that represents all that is. When I put fire to that smoking mixture I send air that has been a part of the water from within my mouth to push that smoke out into the atmosphere that surrounds me. I connect my heart and mind to Great Spirit at this time. It is then in that moment, that I feel I have achieved the sacred alchemy of combining all creative elements: earth, fire, air, water, and Spirit. Anything is possible then.

"Grandson, never forget the Chanunpa was given to humanity to help all people." Grandfather Black Elk reminded me of that statement often throughout his teaching with me. He practiced those words diligently by involving people of all races and creeds in the ceremonies he performed around the world to share its wonders. After my own initiation ceremony in Egypt he reminded me again when we discussed some Sacred Pipes coming from the star and spirit worlds. He believed some Sacred Pipes manifested in our Earth realm as tools to help with our evolution.

The Sacred Pipe, therefore, is a central element in the "Lakota Medicine Way". Almost every major ritual begins or ends with a pipe ceremony in which a shaman's spiritual helpers may be invoked. Smoking the pipe is also an expression of faith in the primary spiritual being, Great Spirit-God. "The pipe was given to the people for their health, welfare, and happiness, and can be utilized to enter the sacred realms where spiritual beings reside. We are able to communicate with Nature then". The pipe ceremony itself utilizes the powers in the cardinal directions, everything that exists above the earth and of the Earth Mother herself, and the eagle and hawk nations.

A true humble shaman, "*icshe wichasa*", knows that there are real powers that live in the directions, "*tatiye topa*". The Lakota word for strong wind is "*tate*". The four directions, or four winds, refers to cosmological powers. These powers are known to be responsible for any significant event, they are considered "*lela wakan*", beyond sacred. It is said Great Spirit gives them their power. An experienced humble shaman knows these beings are very real after all the help they provide, they are not just symbols as others might think. According to my teachers the powers are distinct from each other but are similar in how they work. They have intelligence and wills of their own. They are ancient and are wise beings. It is said the homes of the four winds are in the mountains found in the four quadrants of the Earth Mother. Ordinary stones that materialize in ceremony are signs of their presence. (I have shared some of these seemingly supernatural occurences in each book). The sacred power in the West is said to guard the power of water. A sacred stone looks on from this direction that is black. The sacred power in the North is also said to guard the health of human beings and is known to test those who walk in this sacred manner. A sacred stone looks on from this direction that is red. The sacred power in the East resides where the sun rises and is also said to watch over wisdom and understanding on the earth mother. A sacred stone looks on from this direction that is yellow. The sacred power in the South is said to control the final destiny of all things. His breath is said to give life. A sacred stone looks on from this direction that is white.

QUESTION 10

Q You mentioned in your talk before our ceremony tonight that you are a part of a healer/seer lineage of humble shamans. Could you please help me understand what that means?

TJL Grandfather used to remind me, "Grandson, we can never duplicate the intelligence, energy, and power of Great Spirit, however, we are able to work within the laws of nature in accord with the powers to create what many beings might consider miracles through these 'Sacred Ways'.

A humble shaman in my view, literally enters into the wisdom of the universe via this ancient technology which begins by looking within. Many of these practices date back to the earliest versions of humankind in our present form. A "healer" in this tradition utilizes his or her spiritual allies and powers often accumulated over many years to help others with a physical, spiritual, mental, or emotional issue. A "seer" in this tradition may utilize those same sources to receive guidance regarding what may be the most effective manner to produce a successful healing result if one is possible. A "seer" is often able to view energy in motion to help him or her connect with their spiritual allies during a healing ceremony.

Because these skills are not practiced by the average man Grandfather felt we were born with these talents. I concur, though my specific view is that I retained those skills within the soul that "I am" after many lifetimes.

QUESTION 11

Q Could you tell us how you received the name Redhawk and what it means to you?

TJL Spirits gave me the name in a traditional naming ceremony with Grandfather Black Elk. If you are interested in the details of that experience you can read about it in my first book, "In the Spirit of Black Elk: Preserving a Sacred Way". I've admired Red Hawks for many years and was a part of their rehabilitation process and release back into the wilds when I worked for wildlife rehab as a park ranger. In that space they were red tailed and red shouldered hawks. Sometimes they are perched at the tops of bare trees. Sometimes they are hunched on fence posts after a soaking rain. Other times I see them soaring against the sun and a clear cerulean blue sky. At times they are like missiles shooting down through space to acquire their next meal. While deep in forests I have seen them darting between branches with great speed and dexterity. At times they glide slowly over my head. It seems like they are wherever I am. They are an unusual part of this Sacred Way for me. When I think of a friend and then call them on the telephone, many times they tell me they have just seen a Red Hawk.

I see them in dream-time. When I am there I can hear their piercing cries. I sometimes feel for a few heartbeats that I am soaring with them. I can literally feel the tug of a rising thermal and glimpse the earth from afar. My head feels light. I am confident and coordinated in my new movements through space. My eyes grow huge and become fixed to each side of my head so I can see all around me quite easily. My body feels the muscles and organs located near my center. I am healthy and compact. My wings unfurl and my legs are tucked close to my body. My blood pressure is high and pumping energy throughout my new shape. I feel my lungs fill deeply with air. I am explosive and powerful. When I open my wings I can literally hop into the wind. I am hovering in my extra light body. I can sense the hollow aspects of my bones and feathers. I digest and excrete my food as I have no bladder. I feel perfectly light and effortless. As I ride a burst of wind I can feel the air stream over my extended wings. My smaller feathers buffer any turbulence. I can feel the lifting force pull me up from above. I can sense the rigidity of my spine to center the sturdy aircraft that I am. I pump my wings to increase my speed. Oxygen soaks into my body as I steer with my tail and wing feathers. Soaring…soaring…soaring….I love to soar. I make a wide sweep to my left. Then I slowly make a wide sweep to my right. As I begin to descend I recall my human shape… I can feel again the weight of my arms and legs and torso. I have become a humble man again. I love that too.

Grandfather Black Elk said these words to me on the day of my naming ceremony, "Grandson, you have a new name, you are 'Red Hawk', *Che-tan Lu-ta*." That was all he said, but he was smiling broadly. I think he liked it. Much later, when I asked my spirit helpers in an inipi ceremony what my new name meant, they stated, "A Red Hawk is capable of flying high with the eagles to see great distances. It can even see into the future. A Red Hawk is also capable of maneuvering with quick turns in tight quarters and is very capable of making good decisions in the moment. The red symbolizes fire which represents the living spirit of the people. This fire resides within you."

QUESTION 12

Q Your Grandfather Wallace Black Elk expressed what he thought our true purpose on Earth was in a ceremony I completed with him many years ago. He referred to this topic as our four reasons for being. Could you refresh my memory as to what his thoughts were on that matter if you can?

TJL Grandfather felt there were four reasons for being human that we needed to acquire and exhibit:

* generosity: was considered one of the highest virtues of a true human being.

* courage: to engage in life, whatever you are faced with. This becomes especially important to interface with the highest powers of the universe to move forward on your own "Sacred Way".

* wisdom: was acquired through experiences in a focused often intense interaction with Nature.

* children: there was nothing more important than having children or teaching and nurturing the next generation.

QUESTION 13

Q How did an ex-park ranger like yourself become a sacred man?

TJL That story is revealed in my first two books, "In the Spirit of Black Elk: Preserving a Sacred Way" and "An Angel and a Shaman". The short version is that one of my sons was found to be blind in one of his eyes around the age of five, and after performing a ceremony with another of my mentor's Red Buffalo that restored his sight in that eye, he and Grandfather Black Elk encouraged me to enter this "Sacred Way". When Grandfather spoke to me directly about believing that a humble shaman was born with these gifts and that his spirit guides had advised him to teach me I realized what a unique opportunity I had been given. My mentors encouraged me to practice my skills in family stone-people-lodges where they knew I would gain my confidence to proceed. Still it is like jumping off a cliff to take those skills to the next levels. It just so happened that I had been given a perfect place to perfect my skills while living in a wilderness park setting. Even with all that their came with it a higher sense that I could possibly help others with this knowledge and that eventually occurred. After my initiation in the Great Pyramid I realized my own spirit guide, my angel, had come to let me know she would help me every step of the way. My pursuit of understanding soul from my past lives ran parallel to my perfecting my shaman skills and understanding how I could utilize this wisdom. Then if you read my books, my hanbleychas in the wilds were of supreme importance in acquiring the powers necessary to carrying out what Great Spirit had in mind for me.

QUESTION 14

Q You mentioned earlier how beneficial you felt the practice of meditation could be for most human beings. Would you help me understand your commitment to meditation?

TJL Meditation from my viewpoint is a means of promoting peace and harmony within the person attempting the practice. It is a means of opening oneself to the universe and Great Spirit. The formal practice of sitting meditation was taught by the Buddha over 2,500 years ago. It was an oral tradition that taught both a gentleness toward oneself and an appreciation for our world. The very basic act of finding a quiet space for contemplation is at the heart of any form of this practice. Some people meditate on a question or problem. Some people are able to achieve a higher consciousness after focusing their body and mind in a tranquil manner on nothing in particular. Posture while sitting with an erect back is important to some. Breathing in a specific way can be important to others. Quiet your mind and heart and see what happens for you as you dedicate some time each day to making this special connection with our universe.

QUESTION 15

Q Could you please help me understand the concept of interconnectedness?

TJL Nature is an organic interconnected whole in which no one thing can be considered totally separate from any other thing. We are all a part of a constantly changing flow of energy that manifests to form different dimensional states that interpenetrate one another even right where we sit tonight. We are all one family connected by Great Spirit. During traditional stone-people-lodges, "to all my relations" is spoken as a greeting and an ending to each part of the ceremony to celebrate and honor our connection to each other and Great Spirit and there is no better space to understand this concept than a stone-people-lodge.

QUESTION 16

Q Would you please tell us what your angel has shared with you about the true genesis of human beings on Earth?

TJL No longer should we be left with the notion that we were created fully formed in a nebulous garden only several thousand years ago. Nor should we adhere to the Darwinian model that we crawled out of the primordial ooze and evolved from the ape. Seven divine benefactors, angels from the highest order, are the true co-creators of humanity, as directed by Great Spirit. Other subordinate levels of planetary angels, and angels associated with the sun and moon also played a part in our creation millions of years ago. Each of the original seven archangels was responsible for providing the light and life essential to the first seven groups of human beings created on Earth. Those archangels were powerful, mighty, and of the highest order sent here to not only help create humankind, but also assist with the creation of the animal, vegetable, and mineral kingdoms that would follow. Those kingdoms followed us, not preceded us, as other erroneous texts have stated.

QUESTION 17

Q Would you please clarify for us what your angel meant when she referred to the first manifestation of human beings on Earth?

TJL She refers to the first human forms that came about through their creation by seven archangels developed in seven sacred locations on Earth. These prototypes were realized through the direct utilization of the divine essence from the astral bodies of the archangels. Those first manifestations were ethereal, sexless, semi-spirits, with no minds, intelligence, or will, and fell far short of their intended goal.

QUESTION 18

Q Would you please clarify for us what your angel meant when she referred to the second manifestation of human beings on Earth?

TJL She refers to the second manifestation of human forms on Earth that came about through the seven archangels incarnating into the non-physical bodies of the first manifestations in their attempt to improve many of the deficiencies of those first proto-types. The second manifestations took on more physical characteristics acquired directly through the archangels, however, most of the first manifestation's deficiencies remained and they would be considered semi-human by today's standards. These beings perished within the natural process of evolution.

QUESTION 19

Q Would you please clarify for us what your angel meant when she referred to the third manifestation of human beings on Earth?

TJL She refers to the third manifestation of human forms created by the seven archangels which must be divided into three separate groups of development. The first wave of this third manifestation of human beings were asexual, egg bearing, and still very ethereal beings. The second wave of this third manifestation of human beings was much like the first wave with the exception that they were bisexual and eventually androgynous. The third wave of this third manifestation of human beings could finally be considered the first physical race on our planet. Their development took place on seven sacred locations within the huge continent of Lemuria. A male and female gender was soon established there. Procreation became the chosen avenue to populate the Earth by the third manifestation of these human beings with the exception of the purest of this manifestation who were directly created from the seven archangels. This group became the first semi-spiritual race on Earth with an awareness of the divine wisdom passed along to them. Many of the beings that came onto the Earth through procreation degenerated into self-worship, sorcery, idolatry, and superstition during that time. Lemuria eventually would disintegrate into smaller units of land and new lands began to rise all over the Earth especially in our equatorial regions due to a decrease in the Earth's velocity of rotation. This action caused tilts in every direction causing water to flow towards the poles which then became subject to submersion as well. Most of the third manifestations of human beings perished under the seas at this time.

QUESTION 20

Q Would you please clarify for us what your angel meant when she referred to the fourth manifestation of human beings on Earth?

TJL She refers to the fourth manifestation of human forms created by the seven archangels which took place within the continent of Atlantis on seven sacred locations. These human beings would be considered giants by today's standards. The fourth manifestation proto-types were endowed with great Earth wisdom, beauty, and strength. However, because of the nature of our material plane the highest intentions of the seven archangels were transformed into impure intelligence by many of this manifestation. A struggle ensued between those beings that identified with Great Spirit and true wisdom, and those beings whose deity became matter itself. The holy ones practiced meditation, could control the elements, and had the ability to read their future in the stars. The unholy ones became sorcerers, black magicians, and sexually obsessed self-worshipers. They birthed what might be considered monsters and giant animals due to their sexual intercourse between species. Most of these proto-types were destroyed during the last great axial disturbance on the planet when major portions of the huge continent of Atlantis disappeared under the sea.

QUESTION 21

Q Would you please clarify for us what your angel meant when she referred to the fifth manifestation of human beings on Earth?

TJL She refers to the fifth manifestation of human forms which is us. The archangels instructed us regarding consciousness, ethics, morals, and all aspects of living. They became known as the creators, builders, watchers, preceptors, destroyers, overseers, protectors, and rulers throughout our true prehistory and sacrificed themselves through reincarnation to provide the inner intelligence for mankind to fully develop as the divine beings that we are. When these benefactors incarnated as Kings and other elect of civilizations they directed the minds of men to the invention and perfection of all arts and sciences. They invented letters, the alphabet, and languages. They created appropriate laws, legislature, architecture, medicinal uses of plants, various modes of magic, and developed agriculture, out of their tremendous love for us.

This teaching occurred during our infancy after the last pole shift when major portions of Atlantis were destroyed along with the majority of the fourth manifestations of human beings.

QUESTION 22

Q Being a person of color, I am curious if you have any information about the complexion of the different manifestations of human beings that have come before our own to this point in time?

TJL The first manifestation of human beings complexion was moon colored tending towards yellow and white. The second manifestation of human beings complexion was yellow tending towards gold. The third manifestation of human beings complexion was red. The fourth manifestation of human beings complexion was brown tending towards black. Blue and green complexions were said to also exist at this time and were also destroyed with the majority of the fourth manifestation at the end of that age. The first seven locations of each manifestation of human beings began as one color which soon became mixed through the generation of the species from the fourth manifestation of humanity onward through our fifth manifestation.

QUESTION 23

Q What does it really mean when you refer to our world as being three-dimensional?

TJL Even though our view of space appears to occupy an infinite extension in all directions it can be measured in only three directions independent of one another. Those directions are height, length, and width. Within those three directions we define our dimensions of space as third dimensional space. A humble shaman's viewpoint varies from this status quo perspective because we know our universe to be comprised of multiple dimensions as yet undiscovered by our scientific community but often explored as part of this "Sacred Way".

QUESTION 24

Q Would you please clarify for me the Hindu philosophy which you referred to as "the eternal now"?

TJL The Hindu philosophy of the "eternal now" postulates a universe in which there is neither a before nor after, there exists just one present, which can be known or unknown. I am grateful to this community of sacred men and women who have protected the real history of the planet and continue to do so.

QUESTION 25

Q I have heard you mention Thoth on more than one occasion out of Egyptian prehistory. What more can you share with us about this being that you admire so deeply?

TJL He is known as a master of our greatest mysteries and therefore a perfect candidate for this conversation. I believe him to be one of the reincarnated elect that I have spoken to you about that have been a part of the hidden real history of planet Earth. He becomes prominent as Thoth during the time of Atlantis. He was known as an expert record keeper, shaman, and architect. He is thought to be one of the builders responsible for the Great Pyramid which became and remains a great temple of initiation with the likes of Jesus, Solomon, Apolonius, and many others too numerous to mention who took their initiations within it. It is said it was also built to help balance the great axial disturbances the Earth had experienced during this fourth world age. He is said to have ruled many thousands of years over the gigantic continent of Atlantis, South America, Central America, and Egypt, where he was deified as the "God of Wisdom". He is said to have been the holder of the "Key of Life", which freed him from being bound by death. His search for truth within our material realm took him to many unknown dimensions and worlds until time was non-existent and space blended into nothingness. The wisdom of the "great whole" was his to bring forth into our consciousness. When his knowledge and wisdom

were subverted by those people who had manipulated his knowledge for selfish ends they eventually
were swept under the seas. Much of his wisdom
was preserved for future ages on Emerald Tablets
of an indestructible nature to be reintroduced on
the planet at the proper time.

QUESTION 26

Q You have mentioned the Emerald Tablets on more than one occasion as having historical significance for the future of our planet. What more can you tell us about the Emerald Tablets?

TJL When the time came for the great Master of Mysteries, Thoth, to leave our Earth realm, he placed in the Great Pyramids his records and certain devices to protect them. The Emerald Tablets are a part of those records said to be made of an indestructible substance to be utilized by humanity when we are ready for them. They are said to have been written in words that respond to attuned thought waves, releasing the associated mental vibration in the mind of the reader revealing the wisdom Thoth left behind.

It is said the Emerald Tablets surfaced as a talisman during the second millennium B.C. to certain locations of high wisdom and knowledge on our planet, and were temporarily placed under a Mayan altar rumored to have been at Chichen Itza around 1925 by the "Brotherhood" that I have also spoken to you about. Part of my work revealed in my books to that sacred city, was to explore that possibility which I was associated with in a past lifetime.

QUESTION 27

Q I found your teaching about what happens to a human being after death fascinating and wonder if you would review that information with us tonight?

TJL I am happy to give you the information my angel shared with me to help you live your life in an authentic manner. When the death of a human being takes place the force which holds our cells together is withdrawn and our physical bodies disintegrate. The soul leaves the body it occupied during that lifetime. The influence of your higher mind is withdrawn. Your astral body rises from your physical body like a cloud of thin luminous vapor. As the cord that connects the two becomes thinner it eventually breaks. This event is sometimes visible to those still living. Eventually this astral body is discarded and it disintegrates. Your whole life from infancy to old age passes before your mental vision. Many events are made clear as picture after picture passes before the departing soul. Often times a whole life is better understood. A semi-conscious blissful state then sets in and the lower or instinctive mind dissolves. Each soul awakens when only the highest aspects of the intellect and spiritual mind remain. Your soul then passes to the plane within the astral world suitable to its progress and development. Preparation eventually begins there for your next incarnation. Souls that reach the higher planes often spend more time out of body between lives. After a soul attains a certain level of consciousness past lives are revealed and more choices occur. There are numerous planes of disembodied existence. The highest of those cannot be described while in a material body, however, they are often confused with what some call heaven. The lowest astral planes are very similar to Earth life without the limitations.

QUESTION 28

Q What is "cosmic consciousness"?

TJL My angel described "cosmic consciousness" as a vast coalescing of humanities collective intentions on Earth, with the cumulative possibility of interacting and changing physical matter. It is a highly ordered viable energetic action capable of transforming our world in the blink of an eye after our collective thoughts reach a tipping point. As I have taught you thoughts have mass.

QUESTION 29

Q What medicinal herbs were available to you and the medicine men and women you were with when you were roaming the hills and gullies of Pine Ridge with your mentors?

TJL The subject of ethno-botany is one I thoroughly enjoy. While I was working as a ranger/naturalist in the backcountry of San Diego, California I gave many walks and lectures having to do with plants. One of the most popular walks I led in those years was one in which we toured our park acreage for not only medicinal herbs but wild edibles which we would prepare together as a group and have a feast to conclude our fun. I am happy to share what I remember regarding medicinal plants around the Pine Ridge Reservation. Snake bite was treated with a poultice of snakeroot, plantain, purple cornflower, and white ash. Breathing difficulties were treated with skunk cabbage to open airways. Sunflowers were utilized to fight colds. Sycamore was utilized as a laxative when an individual was constipated. Willow leaf and bark was utilized to relieve fever. Sage tea was utilized like we might utilize a nutrition drink derived from the extremely aromatic variety of white sage that grew there. For more specific information I recommend you contact a local "pejuta wichasa", a medicine person who utilizes medicinal herbs as part of their healing practice there.

QUESTION 30

Q Is there any other information about stones that you may have discovered that would support what you were taught about stones by your Native teachers?

TJL The stone-nation is a perfect example of one of the many other life forms most people disregard. This is a big mistake. The stone-nation has long reminded humble shaman's of how important all life is. The stones are our record keepers and help us in many ways. Their communication and powers are remarkable. Human beings must let go of their spiritual arrogance to connect with the non-human members of our planetary family. They must learn to listen to the many voices of Great Spirit found throughout the natural world. Most human beings are not willing to believe that a stone can possess an intelligence that allows it to perform work that is beyond the intellect of many. Lapis exillis was a stone that many believe started the Holy Grail dialogue. It was said to have fallen from the heavens during the years when the Knights Templar had great prominence around our planet. It was rumored to contain powers over sickness and aging. Historians such as De Mirville wrote about stones that walked, spoke, delivered oracles and even sang "In Days of Miracles" and "Memores of the Academy of Sciences". Pausanias thought Greeks to be stupid for worshipping stones until he witnessed some of the activities described above. Orpheus writes of a stone that was heavy, hard, and black that "had the gift of speech".

When he tried to caste it away he reported in his records that it made "the cry of a child". Helanos foretold the ruin of Troy via a stone such as this.

Grandfather taught me many truths about stones. On our way to Egypt he recounted his story about the stones he wore in a pouch on his belt during his World War II scouting days. On one occasion behind enemy lines near the Great Pyramid, his stones saved he and his men's lives by alerting him to enemy traffic nearby. While we were in ceremony inside the King's Chamber within the Great Pyramid he handed me that pouch of stones for the first time, and I could feel their hearts beat! There always seemed to be a cosmic teaching for me around the next corner and I am gratefull for help from all of Nature.

QUESTION 31

Q What can you tell us about the "ghost dance" and did you ever have a chance to dance it at any of the revivals I have heard about?

TJL The "ghost dance" was a movement that spread across many western tribes around 1890. Those who took part were told their participation would help to bring about their former freedom and glory which would restore the Earth to a Golden age before the arrival of the "white nation". The movement originated with a vision from a prophet whose name was Wovoka. His followers were instructed not to tell white people that

Jesus was upon the Earth. He claimed to have seen him in a cloud where he had also viewed the dead as alive again. He believed by dancing this round dance until a trance state was reached that the dead would return in the fall or spring. He claimed there would be no more sickness and everyone would be young again. By the fall of 1890 it was said 20 thousand Native Americans had participated. In light of all the broken treaties, betrayals, starvation, sickness, and death, it is no wonder it spread like wildfire for a short time. I have never participated in such a dance. I believe the vision that Wovoka experienced was a result of astral travel to the astral plane. It is a vision some native peoples experience upon their departure to the astral plane after death to the so called "happy hunting ground" just as many others create their own view of heaven.

QUESTION 32

Q You mentioned our countries "manifest destiny" policy tonight in regards to the eventual demise and way of life of many Native Americans. What was that policy specifically and do you have any other information about it?

TJL Manifest destiny was a belief put forward by the United States government that divine providence gave our government the right to occupy the entire continent, even if that meant the eventual destruction and pushing of the former occupants aside. The slaughter of Native Americans became a direct result in the extreme. Before the arrival of Columbus to North America some estimate that as many as 20 million first peoples inhabited the continent. After the European invasion only a third of that number remained. By 1800 that number has been estimated at 500 thousand. By 1930 only 250 thousand remained. Medicine men and women were overwhelmed with the onslaught of unknown diseases such as chicken pox, diphtheria, whooping cough, measles, small pox, scarlet fever, tuberculosis, typhoid fever, influenza, and cholera. Many tribes lost 75 percent of their populations after contact, and others completely disappeared off the face of the Earth.

QUESTION 33

Q You mentioned in our healing ceremony tonight that a humble shaman is sometimes required to leave his physical body to acquire information from other realms to help someone with a specific problem or sickness. You referred to it as astral travel. Could you share anything more with us about that mode of travel?

TJL The process that I was involved with during those moments is commonly referred to as astral travel. It is accomplished through the use of a person's astral body, a less dense replica of a person's physical body that resides on the astral plane. The astral plane is separated from our physical material plane, not by distance or direction. It is separated by a difference in the octave of vibration. In the physical plane we have only three dimensions; height, width, and breadth. No matter what direction we move in we are traveling in one of those ways. Wherever the material plane exists the astral plane exists also, separated only by curves, angles, and vibration. To move to the astral plane you have to focus your attention there. Thought is instantaneously creative there. What you are thinking becomes manifest instantly therefore it is imperative that you remain in control of your thoughts. In the material plane you think in terms of time, space, and distance. In the astral plane there is no distance, no direction, no up, no down, no North, no South, no East or no West. Outside of the material plane you are free of it.

You are outside of time, and the dimensions of the material world. Limitation is in the material plane.

QUESTION 34

Q I have heard you utilize the word "nirvana" on several occasions and I wonder if you would explain again what "nirvana" means?

TJL Nirvana is the realization and experience of the "non-self-nature and oneness of the universe". Buddha taught that it resulted in the extinction of all karma forming behavior, especially the need to continue with successive incarnations.

QUESTION 35

Q If you could choose one document out of pre-history that you could thoroughly study for the benefit of humankind what would that document be and why?

TJL The "Mirror of Futurity" is a secret book in which all cycles within infinite time are recorded. This work is ascribed to Pesh-hun Narada. It is supposed to furnish humanity with all specific calculations of all past cycles as well as all future cycles. I would love to have access to this very real book which my angel tells me is still in existence within the Hindu hierarchy of sacred men.

QUESTION 36

Q If I asked you what was the most important thing for human beings to pay attention to while we live our lives on this material plane, what would that be?

TJL The most important thing for any human being to pay attention to is the nurturing, growth, and advancement of their soul. Knowledge about the human soul and the powers it confers upon mankind will allow us to move steadily towards our enlightenment. We are really spiritual beings living in physical bodies each steadily advancing towards perfection through the unfoldment of our soul.

QUESTION 37

Q Love seems to be a central theme of your teaching regarding what you refer to as a "Sacred Way". Do you have anything else you would like to add to that concept?

TJL The last great avatar to walk on this earth known as Jesus the Christ also advocated the importance of every human being experiencing the sacred aspect of love. He shared that if we each loved each other truly all our difficulties would disappear. This simple concept remained abstract to the majority of human beings at that time and consequently no cosmic consciousness shift occurred. At the center of my teaching is that love transcends all other teachings on the planet and is the most powerful aspect of being human. It is true all we really ever needed was love and yet the simplicity of that statement remains elusive. At the very heart of our progress as human beings can be found the true nature of love and I am hopeful one day most people will understand and truly love the Earth and each other.

QUESTION 38

Q What can you tell us about the true age of the Great Pyramid?

TJL Egyptologists have erroneously dated the Great Pyramid to be approximately 5-6 thousand years old. Scientists from our era have dated it at least 10 thousand years old based on striation marks found at its base from the last great flood to have occurred at that time. Because stone cannot be carbon dated Egyptologists are holding to their limited historical time frame which fits a rather condensed view of historical time and skewed religious texts. My angel has shared with me that the Great Pyramid and Sphinx are nearly 80 thousand years old.

QUESTION 39

Q "In the Spirit of Black Elk: Preserving a Sacred Way" you describe a sarcophagus that you and your Grandfather Black Elk meditated within, while inside the King's Chamber of the Great Pyramid, in Egypt. I have also been to that chamber and I am curious if you have any further information regarding that sarcophagus that you might be willing to share?

TJL You are probably already aware that the entrance to the Kings Chamber within that Great Pyramid is not large enough to allow a solid one piece stone sarcophagus that size to be a part of that room. Either the King's Chamber was designed around it or a lost technology allowed it to be placed there in some other manner. Another interesting part of that mystery is that no one knows what may have happened to its top piece which has been missing from that room since man's first entry. Grandfather and I each spent a short time meditating within it. We felt at that time like it may have been part of another kind of ancient vision quest experience. He stated it reminded him of several Lakota vision quest pits that were not much larger. My angel had this to say about that sarcophagus when I had time to check in on the matter after returning home. She states that during ancient initiations the candidate represents God or Great Spirit during his or her stay within the sarcophagus itself. During this time they become like an energizing ray of light entering into the womb of Nature. When they emerged on the following morning they represented the resurrection of life after the transition we call death. The candidate's figurative death lasted two days in which they survived several tests by the hierarchy involved.

QUESTION 40

Q What more can you tell us about the Upanishads which you spoke of in terms of being a very important ancient text "In the Spirit of Black Elk: Preserving a Sacred Way" and "An Angel and a Shaman?

TJL It is one of our oldest wisdom sources from India expressing the highest truths of Hindu Philosophical Thought. It has survived in partial form several of the devastations that have occurred at the end of each of the worlds discussed in my first two books. "Upanishads" is usually translated as "esoteric doctrine", however, the most precise translation of "Upanishads" according to my angel is "the conquest of ignorance by the revelation of secret spiritual knowledge". The highest purpose of this material was to explain that the subject and object of all being and knowing are one and the same, Great Spirit, which they referred to as Brahman, the One Self, the only true reality.

QUESTION 41

Q I have recently begun to study the Kabala and I wonder if you have ever studied that material and if so do you have any idea where it originated?

TJL I studied the Kabala almost twenty years ago for a short time. I believe many people have benefited from its wisdom teachings over many years even though it is a fairly recent document in terms of earth history. My angel explains the Kabala most likely originated many centuries before the Christian era within an ancient wisdom religion in

Central Asia which descended from India, China, and Egypt and eventually came through Abraham into Palestine.

QUESTION 42

Q What is your take on rampant greed and money acquisition at any cost becoming our civilization's central focus these days at the apparent expense of all else?

TJL An old proverb comes to my mind, "What does it profit a man if he gains the whole world, but loses his soul? Integrity, moral courage, compassion, truth, beauty, and love cannot be purchased and those individuals involved in what you speak about will likely have to come back several lifetimes to understand fully that we are really here to realize Great Spirit in all things and advance our souls along our paths towards perfection each life we lead.

QUESTION 43

Q You quoted an ancient source within our ceremony tonight "If we are to become truth, we have to live truth". Who said it, and what can you tell me about that human being?

TJL The man who said it was a pharaoh and ancient wisdom holder. Aknaton made that statement during his tumultuous reign over all of Egypt. After what he called his great illumination he decreed that God was in fact one "Great Spirit" not a multiplicity of lesser gods as had been formerly taught by the Egyptian priesthood.

From that moment forward he devoted all his time and personal wealth to the development of this monotheistic view throughout his lands. He built temples and shrines to this "Great Spirit" and attempted to eradicate his people's erroneous beliefs. The priesthood that had been living quite well under the old belief system had him killed, however, his wisdom lives on within these words and that policy.

QUESTION 44

Q Would you please share with us what you know
to be true about crop circles, are they real or are
they a hoax?

TJL I have been fascinated by the very real phenomenon referred to as crop circles for many years
though I have not had the opportunity as yet to
explore any examples in person. These mostly
geometrical shapes have been appearing in crop
fields since the early 1970's and I hypothesize that
they appeared before that date as well though they
went unrecorded. The crops that they appear in

are usually not harmed in any way as their stems are bent and they continue to ripen in their altered positions. This phenomenon has been reported in many countries, especially in England where several unrelated hoax circles were carried out to attempt to explain away the authentic circles. No one to this point in time seems to have deciphered the meaning behind these authentic images. When they do appear they are sometimes accompanied by small lights similar to those that are seen within the stone-people-lodge ceremonies that I have helped facilitate for many years. Some of the crop circles have been noted to include an unusual sound by those who have witnessed the lights working in the crops. As is the case with any phenomenon that science cannot explain the intricate designs of these unique images are often swept under the proverbial rug by the scientific community. My angel explained that Nature which geometrizes universally in all her manifestations not only in the primordial plane but also the phenomenal plane is actually carrying out the work herself. It would seem as though the very "soul of our planet" is attempting to educate us in some manner which is an area of awareness most people are not familiar with, that our planet is a living entity.

QUESTION 45

Q I have heard many people speak about karma and I sort of have a general idea what it means, but I wonder if you would clarify the concept for us tonight?

TJL Karma is the science of effects produced by causes. It comes from the Sanskrit word "Kri", meaning to do or to act. It refers directly to the effect of all of your actions in life. Many people and religions are confused by the Law because they erroneously believe that punishment is central to how it works. Karma is simply that which comes from an action.   It applies to stars, planets, suns, and nations, as well as human beings.   If our actions set up a condition in our lives then events will appear as the effect of the cause put in motion. The avatar Jesus attempted to simplify the law by stating "As you sew, so shall you reap". He taught that we are each responsible for our lives. My angel explained that Jesus also shared that Karma is sometimes carried over to a person's next incarnation. She states that there is a plane of the Divine Mind where the causes we set in motion reside, before they materialize in our lives. A balancing of all causes occurs there.

QUESTION 46

Q Would you share with us what happened surrounding the Viet Nam Veteran several of us
asked you to look in on the next time you got out
to Orcas Island? We were concerned about him
hurting himself or another being based on the
state of mind we found him in.

TJL The gentleman you speak of was also a Native
American in addition to being a Viet Nam veteran.
When I heard about him falling on hard times I
naturally scheduled a time I could get out to where
he lived to find out what had occurred. As it

turns out he had been acting as a very competent care taker for an elder who had lived out there for many years. Unfortunately he and the elder had never put into writing what would happen to his caretaker after he himself passed over, which had just occurred. Apparently the surviving relatives asked the caretaker to leave the property he had lived on for many years. This had apparently made an unstable situation even more precarious when the caretaker decided he was not going to leave peacefully. By the time I arrived on the scene he was well armed and quite surly after drinking all day and threatening anyone nearby with violence. I brought my drum and chanunpa to his Viet Nam style hooch sitting with a million dollar view on the side of a mountain and began to immediately get all the facts of the scene. My drum took over and soon the caretaker had joined me in song though his many guns were still quite evident. I agreed to sleep over on that property that evening and found myself well within his firing range. I explained to him we would do a ceremony next evening after he had gone through 24 hours of purification from the alcohol he had consumed the day before. I prayed throughout the day for a solution. After taking him out for breakfast the next mid-day we settled upon how his ceremony would go which included a sacred pipe and some ceremonial cleansing. After several healing songs which I sang and drummed my angel asked me to sprinkle water over the care-taker's eyes. This movement caused the caretaker to comment that black flies were leaving his eyes. What we saw together were hundreds of black flies leaving his physical being. He went from an out of control being to his old self during that happening. Last I heard he was living in a subsidized old folks home very peacefully.

QUESTION 47

Q Could you share your view of reincarnation with us tonight?

TJL The concept of reincarnation recognizes that the life of the soul is what is paramount as we live our physical lives from lifetime to lifetime on Earth. The soul eventually discovers the consciousness that we do not die in the sense of those who believe we live only one physical life, and death is our singular end. The mature soul realizes that when we leave our material bodies behind, we will eventually occupy a new body each lifetime, until the perfection of our soul is realized. The advanced soul sees physical life for what it really is and understands the highest aspects of being human are reached through reincarnation and the unfoldment of soul.

QUESTION 48

Q Would you talk about the spirit Eagle that comes to the interior of your stone-people-lodge ceremonies?

TJL Poets write about time, how it moves, and what it means. But it is a shaman, who experiences eternity compressed into a sublime moment of connecting their energy to a spiritual ally. It is in that sacred space and time where new knowledge and power to help others may be acquired. Various elements may be part of that acquisition such as isolation, no food, no water, sacred songs, sage, sweet-grass, cedar, frequency of a drumbeat, a Chanunpa ceremony, a feather, a sacred stone, fire, earth, air, water, and other potential doorways. Most important is a receptive being with an open heart and mind.

I first noticed the Eagle's deep connection to Grandfather Black Elk when, before his first overnight stay with us at our home within Wilderness Gardens Preserve, I spotted an eagle in flight a few moments before we ran into each other. I noticed eagles in flight almost every time we were about to meet. Many times we were in areas where this kind of sighting would be considered unusual. It became so commonplace for me to see them I began to look for what he called "his scouts" prior to our teaching sessions and ceremonies. I would usually see an eagle flying near the vicinity of wherever he was about to make an appearance. During my years of working with him directly this went on, and his only comment when I brought them up to him, was that "he had sent his scouts out to look for me". On this particular occasion, four years into my training, after he had observed me viewing one of "his scouts" circling high above him, he shared this story in the stone-people-lodge:

"Grandson, many years ago I was driving along a highway and something caught my eye along the side of the road. Before me was an eagle that had been shot. It was barely alive with a damaged wing. I began to pray to Tunkashila to see what I could do to help. I tried to fix the wing and stop the bleeding but about half way through my prayer I realized that eagle had died in my arms. The next time we did a ceremony I took that eagle body into the lodge to ask what had happened. I know you have experienced many supernatural moments already regarding this path, and so you will understand that during our prayer there was a flash of lightening, and the spirit of that eagle appeared before us. It fanned me and touched me with a human hand and thanked me for what I had done. I wept as it gave me a physical feather that I still have in my medicine case. That eagle spirit said it would be hovering over me. It said it would be in front of me, on both sides of me, and underneath me. 'Spirit' made me that promise. During that ceremony I asked *Tunkashila,*'Creator' what had happened? I then heard what sounded like a rifle shot. I thought one of the stones in the lodge had exploded. Then I realized a bullet had gone through that eagle's body again. It ricocheted around the interior of that lodge and bounced off one of the saplings that was holding the blankets up for our stone-people-lodge structure. I had part of my answer then. Four days later while driving the same road where I had found that eagle I noticed a pickup truck alongside the road and a man lying by a rifle. When I asked the old people that had been drawn there also by that sight, what had happened, they told me that they saw the man try to shoot an eagle that had been sitting in the field and when he went to get his rifle out of his pickup, the rifle went off and killed him. Grandson, I knew then it was the same man and was reminded once again of the great powers of these ways." After that ceremony I never wondered about the eagles that I always saw around Grandfather again.

When I went on my hanbleycha to Alaska several years later, I had one of my most inspirational moments since beginning this journey meeting the eagles at Eagle Council Grounds along the Chilkat River. During my hanbleycha on that sacred ground they came to me to give me their help. (Details about that vision quest can be found in my first book). I remember wondering if my relationship to Grandfather and his teaching had created my connection to them. Eagle and Red Hawk spirits have helped in the healing aspects of my work on many occasions ever since. The physical altar that a "humble shaman" presents is the arrangement of objects, prayer ties, and spirit robes, utilized at the onset of a ceremony always presented with a Sacred Pipe. This altar might also display the powers that are included from other realms that are associated with that particular "humble shaman" in some other physical form.

During the building of our first stone-people-lodge on our land in the Pacific Northwest with the help of several friends, as if on cue, a bald eagle flew over our heads and circled exactly four times above our lodge, and then disappeared over the tree line. I knew in that moment Grandfather was also pleased with our sacred architecture. Over my years of helping him with his teaching we built lodges in many environments, and on almost every one of those occasions we were blessed by a spirit eagle appearance.

Native legends state the eagle and condor fly higher than any other birds and are often considered to be closer to Great Spirit because of this aspect. They are looked upon as the messengers for our prayers and are synonymous with the spiritual realm. I often encounter spirit eagles during healing ceremonies and on many occasions am able to literally hear them thump through the roof of a stone-people-lodge to offer their assistance in some manner. Sometimes I can see them in the inner expanses of that sacred space. For me they have come to represent spiritual illumination and the intelligence of Great Spirit paying a visit to our proceedings.

QUESTION 49

Q Why is there evil in our world?

TJL The linking of pure Spirit with impure matter is the cause that has led to that effect.

QUESTION 50

Q What is your perspective regarding the Earth up to the creation of mankind and can you speak in terms of a time line?

TJL The planets of our solar system came into being several billions of years after the "big bang" estimated to have occurred approximately 13.5 billion years ago. I consider Great Spirit to be responsible for that event. At that time stars were born and super nova explosions 200 million years later created all elements that we currently are aware of such as uranium, gold, and copper. The planets were formed, approximately 5.3 billion years ago-including Earth. 4.6 billion years ago it is believed our planet was comprised of a molten lava crust and core and our magnetic field began to form. Our atmosphere at that time is said to have been composed of helium and hydrogen. 100 million years later, due to constant volcanic activity, our atmosphere became mostly steam and carbon dioxide which eventually condensed into vast areas of water. Over the next billion years bacteria evolved which began to consume the carbon dioxide and excrete oxygen and nitrogen. That oxygen eventually became a part of the air we currently breathe. A billion years later land masses began to form changing ocean currents and climate which included the formation of ice. Life is said to have become complex then and the Earth became ready for human occupation at that time. 500 million years ago our ozone layers formed. 160 million years later our first human prototypes came into being during the first manifestation of humanity and 60 million years later plants and amphibeans moved from the sea to land.

QUESTION 51

Q I have heard you describe a specific time in our prehistory as the "Golden Age" on our planet. What can you tell me about it?

TJL It was a time when "the divine seven archangels and other helping angels walked the Earth in bodies and mixed freely with mortals during the third manifestation of humankind. They made their homes in a real physical location while occupying those bodies. That land became known as Shamballa. Shamballa was an island surrounded by water where the Gobi desert now exists. The

Divine Benefactors who were responsible for the creation of the third manifestation of humankind lived there with remnants of that third race from Lemuria after the sinking of that continent. They were responsible for imparting nature's most mysterious secrets to mankind.

QUESTION 52

Q Would you be willing to sum up what you referred to as a humble shaman's journey for us tonight?

TJL True humble shamans are human beings who have journeyed through life and have overcome circumstances and set-backs just like each of you. We have learned from our experiences over many lifetimes to help us understand the universal laws that the divine consciousness manifests through. My personal goal has been to share my knowledge whenever appropriate. A humble shaman masters the powers and forces unknown to many in order to reach a heightened state of spiritual and mental attunement that allows for a deep connection to Great Spirit. This "enlightened state of a shaman" refers to a condition free of illusion when a shaman's finite consciousness becomes one with the higher powers. It is made possible by the level of advancement of the soul. During this time any one of the "supernatural talents" available to the shaman may be manifested for the purpose of helping another being. This is a temporary sublime condition as opposed to the permanent nature of perfect enlightenment.

QUESTION 53

Q You mentioned prior to our ceremony an environmental disaster that led to the eventual destruction of the Native American societies of the Great Plains. Would you please clarify that statement for me?

TJL I was referring to the intentional mass annihilation of the buffalo. This action became a central focus of the crusade waged against Native Americans of that region by the intrusion of the railroads and the European migration across what was once native land. Native American populations had been dependent upon buffalo for food, shelter, and clothing before their demise. Estimates place 30 million bison roaming North America before 1800. By 1930 only a few hundred bison remained. Entire ecosystems were radically changed within the span of a few years not only affecting the human populations but also the animal, vegetable, and mineral kingdoms surrounding them. In spite of this calamity the buffalo nation lives on within sacred practices such as those associated with the sacred pipe. Buffalo spirit helpers have helped me for many years in this manner and have been a part of many sacred occasion since I began my journey on this "Sacred Way". My story of how four Spirit Buffalo appeared in a cloud formation in the sky above me while I fasted on "Bear Butte" in South Dakota is revealed in my first book, "In the Spirit of Black Elk: Preserving a Sacred Way".

QUESTION 54

Q Could you clarify your statement that thoughts potentially can create?

TJL The mysterious power of a thought at times enables it to produce external perceptible phenomenal results by its own inherent energy. Any thought may potentially manifest itself externally if ones attendant will is concentrated upon it with the proper power and unselfish intent. Thoughts are literally things. They are extremely powerful and can remain in existence long after you have a memory of sending them. An appropriate analogy would be when flowers with a specific scent have occupied a space in your home and then they are removed. You are usually still able to smell their scent in the air long after their physical presence has vanished. So too, are thoughts able to carry power.

QUESTION 55

Q You have mentioned that bear was a spiritual ally of yours. Would you be willing to share anything else with us about that connection?

TJL Grandfather took it upon himself to share with me many different "medicines" that he apparently felt I needed to know about or would be personally holding as a healer and seer. Early on I was very aware I held certain characteristics representative of the bear nation such as my fierce protection for my sons as if they were my bear cubs. I had more than one direct moment of meeting bears in the wild along my own path. I had seen grizzly bears perhaps as close as forty to fifty yards away grazing in the hills on my backpacking excursions into Glacier National Park in Montana. I had also experienced Grizzly Bears at Denali National Park in Alaska from roughly the same distance feasting on salmon. I had several people tell me I was crazy for going into those backcountries without a gun, however, I never felt threatened by any of those bears. When you are with them in that circumstance there is a real aspect to understanding you are a part of the circle of life. I felt my thoughts protected me there and I never represented fear. I also remember having some great bear dreams while there. As I grew on my own "Sacred Way" I realized there were many moments I had morphed into my "bear medicine" utilizing all my strength and courage to accomplish something I may not have been even able to approach without it. I suppose I have been physically intimidating at times when that was called for in the moment. I remember several camp fires Grandfather and I sat around where he explained that "bear medicine men" were some of the most powerful healers of his lineage. He explained that in the old days bear medicine men had the ability to in one motion seal up a wound with their hands. At times this could include the removal of a bullet still in a wound. Red Buffalo also spoke about them, and it was he who gave me my first bear claw for my medicine bag.

Before one of Grandfather's Sun Dances he and I along with one of his nephews had the pleasure of doing a stone-people-lodge with a modern day version of a young bear medicine man. When we arrived at this bear medicine man's property we were immediately escorted out to his stone-people-lodge site which looked to be a small circular clearing adjacent to a sheer rock faced cliff covered in scrub oak and pine. After introductions were made and I settled in to build our fire for the stone-people-lodge ceremony and take on the duties of his fire keeper, the bear medicine man began to exhibit some of the sounds and characteristics of a bear. I could not take my eyes off of him during the approximately two hours of time the stones took to glow their magic quality orange red as we readied for our lodge. He wore a bear skin cloak and often stamped and clawed the Earth. We would be four human beings once inside our lodge praying for a successful Sun Dance. Our stone-people-lodge would not be the usual bent saplings covered with skins or blankets this night. It would be a cave entrance covered with a bear hide door opening to a circular cave about 12 feet in diameter within. On our way in we were asked to anoint our third eyes with a special bear medicine. I had never worked as a fire keeper for such a man before. It was an extremely hot four doors that were special to each of us in many ways and at the end of our time we shared a traditional feast prepared back at his cabin amid tremendous happiness and gratitude for what we knew would be a successful Sun Dance.

QUESTION 56

Q Has the Earth's axis ever gone through a realignment or shift to another position during any of the past ages that you have referred to in your "Sacred Earth" writing?

TJL My angel explains our Earth's axis has shifted on at least four occasions during this fourth incarnation of our planet. The last example of this action occurred when the continent of Atlantis, then a gigantic land area made up of seven large islands began to break apart and disappear under the sea after a massive shift in Earth's axis. This action was followed by the most devastating deluge in Earth's history which has gone through several smaller deluge episodes, the most recent occurring approximately 12 thousand years ago contributing to the remaining Atlantis Island referred to by Plato in his writings, of disappearing under the sea.

QUESTION 57

Q Can you speak to us about what you have learned about healing?

TJL Each of us holds the keys to our own healing and excellent health. Webster's dictionary defines health as a natural condition of wholeness. To help facilitate healing or curing in human beings, I learned over my years of this work that people must be brought back into their natural harmony. This movement sometimes included me suggesting more than one healing modality to reach the state of well-being intended. My spiritual allies sometimes recommended more than one path to achieve a complete cure. As an example, some illnesses might best be eradicated through a physical pathway, while others were best handled through emotional, mental, or metaphysical avenues. A physical modality might include diet or nutritional changes, acupuncture, or the latest treatment through their western physician. An emotional modality might include the use of color, sound, or aroma therapies. A mental modality might include visualization or hypnosis. A metaphysical modality might include shamanic methodologies or simple healing touch. At other times the sacred mystery powers took over and what the patient sought came about with the help of Spirit, sometimes instantly. A sacred level of consciousness and movement was achieved in those moments from what Grandfather called *taku wakan*, the "Great Mystery".

When Grandfather and Red Buffalo stated to me that shamans are each unique in how they go about their work I had no idea how that might take shape for me or how we might differ in our approach to achieving excellent health for those who sought it from us but we were each unique.

I feel a successful healer must be fluid in their movements and decisions with this work moment to moment. A humble man or woman must always be compassionate and reflect love to bring about a positive result. We must strike a balance between the powers and the wisdom we acquire for those asking for help. At times my spiritual allies would inform me that I would not be able to successfully help someone, and the pull on my heart-strings was usually extreme when I informed them I could not help. At other times it was explained to me that a complete healing was possible if certain instructions were followed. Sometimes a complete cure occurred as a result. Other times the instructions given to a seeker by Spirit were not completed and the sought after cure remained elusive.

A humble shaman attempts to live fully in the moment with great joy. There are many times when a successful healing takes place and the harmony of body, mind, and spirit is achieved. In my stone-people-lodge ceremonies, my spiritual allies were honored with 150 red prayer ties on one string, and an additional 23 prayer ties of colors chosen specifically for that occasion, on another string. My angel, though a spirit, required no prayer ties, only positive thoughts and faithful intention. In my healing or curing ceremonies the thank you takes place during the initial ceremony, not a separate ceremony as required by other shamans including my mentor's. That aspect becomes a matter of faith and clarity in the new cause and effect of what will soon occur over time in that healing moment with my helpers. I have found that a person asking for help must want to get well to achieve the healing they require, which is surprisingly not always the case. If my guides pointed this out to me about someone who had asked for help I told them I could not help them and why. It is also important but not always a prerequisite that the person asking for help has knowledge about the sacred mystery powers. There can be no doubts between the healer and the participant in their full intention to bring about a positive result. Each time I was active in this manner, I asked for the universe to send a spiritual helper appropriate for whatever was needed. There was never a time when this did not occur.

I have now been blessed to meet Aboriginal shamans, South American shamans, Central American shamans, Asian shamans, European shamans, African shamans, and of course North American shamans. This communication helped me to understand clearly that there are many approaches to shamanic healing and curing which Grandfather and Red Buffalo reminded me about often. Some involve restoring beneficial energies. Others involve extracting harmful ones. Grandfather used the word "toka" to describe "the enemy" he sometimes encountered while carrying out his work. In the healing process Grandfather and Red Buffalo shared with me, no mind altering substances were utilized in the communication with a shaman's spiritual allies to form a diagnosis or cure. The stones, prayer ties, beat of the drum, sacred songs, sage, sweet-grass, and cedar help a humble shaman connect to the powers necessary to help bring about a positive result. In other cultures psychoactive substances are utilized by the shaman and sometimes the patient to journey between worlds to acquire whatever is necessary for a cure. In our society a physician usually administers a drug on the patient to achieve a result, rather than ingesting it himself. Even in our modern world it is sometimes not known whether the placebo effect creates the cure or the drug itself.

One of the biggest misconceptions about a "humble shaman" is that we normally operate in "non-ordinary reality" most of the time. To be perfectly clear, we operate in "non-ordinary reality" only a small portion of our time. Those shamans that I learned from felt that an experienced shaman operated successfully in both ordinary and non-ordinary realms. They were often active in the economic, social, and political decision making of their communities. This concept was a model for me in my own community work taking leadership roles in social, political, educational, and environmental activities whenever that was feasible.

It always intrigued me why a shaman became a shaman during my years of meeting many of these special people. Their answers varied. Some became shamans because of ancestral lineage. Some were called while in "the dreaming." Some were called through great visions. Some were chosen by other worldly beings. Some simply inherited the mantle from a relative. Many spoke of the joys of solitude. One thread that seemed to tie everyone together was the light I noticed in each shaman's eyes, the light of Great Spirit.

I have witnessed the curing and healing of disease happen in all of the ways mentioned above. One lung cancer victim that asked for my help stands out in my mind as a prime example of how powerful the "sacred mystery powers" could be at any moment. After we finished four doors of an intensely hot stone-people-lodge and Sacred Pipe ceremony, this man crawled out of the stone-people-lodge and coughed violently several times. He then vomited a few feet away from the lodge structure. After several moments of regaining his focus he had this to say about that healing moment, "I then watched my cancer literally move into the bushes beyond the lodge, a sickening dark mass oozing on the ground slowly away from me. I knew at that moment I was cancer free, and it turned out to be so."

QUESTION 58

Q I am of Scandinavian heritage and have always wondered if there was any truth to rumors of there being authentic ancient texts called the "Scrolls of Wisdom" still in existence in that part of the world. Can you shed any light on this subject for me?

TJL They were indeed ancient scrolls that referred to many of the teachings of the archaic ages. Most of them have not survived into our present age and have been considered lost, but my angel says that a few remain that speak to the past and future of humankind via Odin's ravens as shared with the old Norse Gods and Goddesses.

QUESTION 59

Q You have shared with us your teaching about the seven worlds that will accompany the seven incarnations of our planet into our distant future. You have also shared information with us about those worlds and incarnations that have already come about. Is there anything else you can add to that wisdom at this time?

TJL The information that I have shared with you comes from the "Renewal of the World Prophecy". My angel tells me it is an authentic ancient wisdom text which refers to the seventh manifestation of humankind during the seventh incarnation of Planet Earth. The seventh world will be the highest and purest according to this prophecy. Humankind is encouraged to walk step by step to higher knowledge and wisdom culminating in perfection and unity with Great Spirit at that time in our future.

QUESTION 60

Q Is there anything else you can share about the term "taku skan" you spoke about in your books?

TJL That was the original term Grandfather used in describing that which causes all things to move in the universe in reference to my stone that materialized before my eyes. Our world is made up of Spirit which Crazy Horse called "everything everywhere spirit". I refer to this entity as Great Spirit. All spirit forms are referred to as "the world

of the intelligence of being", river, tree, stones, etc.
These all hold a spirit form.

QUESTION 61

Q Could you talk to us about yuwipi and the yuwipi man you met with your Grandfather?

TJL At one of Grandfathers Sun Dances, he introduced me to the great Grandson of the Yuwipi man Horn Chips. Horn Chips was the shaman credited with utilizing his powers to help one of the most powerful warrior chiefs in Lakota history, Crazy Horse.

The man that stood before me was the youngest Yuwipi Wichasa in a centuries long family lineage of Yuwipi men on his Reservation. He was round-faced with long black hair, coffee toned craggy features, and a mustache-which was unusual for the native men I knew. Grandfather had mentioned to me that he hoped I could meet this man if I was able to attend the dance. Though I did not know how old he was then, he appeared to be somewhere around my age, in his thirties. Oregon was a long way from his family farm on South Dakota's Pine Ridge Reservation on the Great Plains. I was told he had been hearing the spirits talk since he was thirteen years old when he received his Yuwipi altar to carry on the family tradition. He, like Grandfather Black Elk, had been instructed by their spiritual allies that the "Chanunpa is for all people". He had begun sharing the ancient Yuwipi ceremony a few years before we met with all people, not just his own.

In the Yuwipi ceremony, 405 tiny translucent stones collected from anthills are traditionally collected and placed inside a gourd made of animal hide. Each one represents an individual Spirit. The Spirits in these stones literally communicate to the Yuwipi man. After being bound by leather thongs and lying face down on a bed of sage, covered with a star blanket, the Yuwipi Wichasa is untied by Spirits at the end of the ceremony. Some Yuwipi ceremonies are about finding something or someone. Some are about healing and curing. Some are about seeing into the future or past. "The power of the stones has been lost by many nations," Grandfather Black Elk stated to me. "When you connect your heart and mind to the intent of the ceremony, anything is possible"

I too had heard several stories about the miraculous healings that had happened in the lives of some of the people who had participated in his ceremonies. I over-heard one woman explain around a campfire that someone with multiple sclerosis had been brought to him in a wheel-chair and was on her feet walking the next day. Horn Chips is credited by many Lakota elders as being the first of this specialized form of powerful doctoring. This young Yuwipi man's great Grandfather had devised the protective charms with the help of his spiritual allies that had made Crazy Horse invincible in battle. This fact was witnessed by many Lakota warriors and shared in their oral histories. According to Grandfather Black Elk, a pure form of this "medicine way" was passed from Horn Chips, to his Grandfather, to his father, and to the man who now sat before me finishing his sage crown, anklets, and wristlets for the Sun Dance about to take place. What made him different than most others in his line of work was what the spirits had told him directly, "The Chanunpa is for all people". I found him to be humble and gracious. On this occasion Grandfather asked me to help this Yuwipi Wichasa into the Sun Dance arbour. I carried his ropes and ties and sacred implements into that sacred space and immediately felt the powers there.

I was happy and humbled to have been asked to do that simple task. That walk with him will always be a special memory for me.

QUESTION 62

Q Could you help me understand the language of songs on our sacred Earth?

TJL Grandfather taught me often about the language of songs of Mother Earth. If we were walking on a trail he would often have me pause to listen to a specific song. He would remind me that there are many songs in this universe. For example, the fire has a song. "Fire shapes and forms all life. Each shape has a song. The stones each have a song. Each one also has a language. The entire Earth Mother also has a song. The water in a river has a song. All trees have a song. There is also a language amongst the trees in this canyon and elsewhere. One man could never know all of the songs. Do you smell that scent in the air? Each one of these trees puts out a particular scent. It acts as a message for other beings like the songs we sing. There are many languages in the natural world. That bird has a song". Spirit gifted Grandfather an eagle song, a buffalo song, a whale song, and many other songs. His relatives have passed down many medicine songs to his family. In many cases they fasted four days and four nights to pray and sometimes their efforts were rewarded with a song that would put them in contact with a spirit.

"When we go to pray in our stone-people-lodges many participants will want help with their problems. So we will sing special songs to help them receive help from the nature spirits. On *Turtle Island,* we could go anywhere and we might find a quiet place and learn a song. We can sit by your river and just enjoy creation. I listen to this bubbling brook and take it into my heart. It becomes a medicine that way. I listen to the wind moving through these massive powerful trees and I am amazed how beautiful it all sounds. Then I listen to all the bird nations here and I fill up on those sounds like a hungry bear cub at his first good meal of spring. I simply enjoy listening to what Spirit might have to say to me through that sound.

The foundation of the way of a humble shaman lies in the fire, rock, water, and plant. As I fill my sacred pipe I listen to the words of that special song".

This pipe filling song is the first ceremonial song that I learned:

Kola lece lecun wo Do it this way my friend

Kola lece lecun wo Do it this way my friend

Kola lece lecun wo Do it this way my friend

E canukitaku yacinku ihecetu ktelo Your
prayer will become reality
Canunpa wanzi yuha elota kecin Whenever
you sit with the pipe
Minksuya opagi o he Always remember me
He canuki ni tunkashila waniang uktelo

QUESTION 63

Q What is your take on the message that a great avatar will appear again on the earth plane sometime in our future?

TJL My angel explains that this will occur during the seventh world of the seventh incarnation of our planet. She also goes on to remind us that the original seven archangels referred to as our divine benefactors have reincarnated as great sages, kings, and civilization leaders within the elect of the third, fourth, and our fifth manifestation of human beings to move us ever closer to our real goal of the perfection that we will reach during the time of the avatar spoken of above.

QUESTION 64

Q I am fascinated by your angel's description of the "Brotherhood" in your first two books. Is there any other information you may have that you would be willing to share at this time?

TJL The men and women who kept the original wisdom and knowledge in tact century after century, from the seven beings my angel has referred to as the Divine Benefactors, were the "Brotherhood", or the "Great Light Brother and Sisterhood", as my angel refers to them. She also recently informed me they only exchange their bodies due to death infrequently, and that they rarely move to the astral world between lives. Though what we call nirvana is accessible to them they do not reach for it as they are committed to the ascension of all of mankind upon planet Earth.

QUESTION 65

Q I am aware you rarely share specific information about phenomena that occur surrounding your healing work, however, I was wondering if you would make an exception tonight surrounding your dragonfly helpers that came to the assistance of a person who had asked for your help with her cancer?

TJL I assume you know the patient or someone who was there? Quite a few years ago, I had a women get in touch with me who stated she had heard rumors through her friends about the mysterious powers of the Native form of healing that I practiced. I explained to her that I was indeed a part of this practice and that after a face to face interview with her I could most likely determine if I could help her or not. After our meeting my guides determined she had great inner strength, courage, endurance, and perseverance to have survived up to the point in time we met. She explained her cancer had left her with tumors too close to her heart for her to proceed with mainstream medicine. I explained that I would be directed by spirit guides to come up with a plan for her and began immediately teaching her what I could about the "Sacred Way" that I practiced. During this preparation time, which included several meetings, I informed her that our process would culminate with a healing stone-people-lodge and sacred pipe ceremony to either bring about a direct result or guide us regarding how to further proceed. Her outlook had been very bleak regarding her continued survival based on what her mainstream physicians had informed her. Her husband explained to me he had a real fear of taking part in a stone-people-lodge healing ceremony because of the heat, so I explained to him he could act as our door keeper and remain outside our inner circle during the time of our lodge but listen from the door to the entire proceeding. This would prove to be an integral piece to this healing. As the time grew near for our ceremony my patient tied her prayer ties as per my instructions and six spirit robes for the powers of the directions, black, red, yellow, white, blue and green. I asked her to put specific thoughts for what needed to happen in each tie. I requested help from several of my friends with the fire and tending of the grounds, and songs that we would sing within the stone-people-lodge that evening. Each of those people were instructed to only include positive thoughts as we proceeded with a very hot four door healing ceremony with

.

the 32 stone-people my guides required. After the final segment of the healing ceremony was complete I asked her husband, my doorman, to open the door and let the cool air into the lodge. As I did so many hundreds of dragonflys came to my patient and surrounded her and all of us. When we exited the lodge they seemed to be everywhere. Her husband who had been a bit fearful about the entire evening spoke up and explained a spirit being had whispered in his ear that his wife would be around living a long time. That woman is still alive to this day after her initial tumors shrunk she found further help with mainstream medicine.

QUESTION 66

Q Is there really a physics to your ceremonies and have you ever done a ceremony with scientists?

TJL I was asked to do a stone-people-lodge ceremony in Central Oregon many years ago with a group of physicists from a nearby university, and a handful of other participants from diverse backgrounds and religious beliefs.

The following is a recounting of my talk with that group as you join us in a circle, around our sacred fire, near the stone-people-lodge, at dusk, under lichen covered oaks and scrub-brush, near a trickling brook. I begin my introduction:

"The Lakota word for "sweat-bath" is inipi.. The root word is ni, which means "to live". Niya means to "breathe". There are many reasons one takes part in the ceremony we will be taking part in tonight. Two reasons seem most important to me, "wicozanni", health, and for "wiconi", life. The literal translation of inipi is "for their life". I take this ceremony very seriously and recommend if you are crawling into one of these you know enough about the person pouring water to feel comfortable with their skills to carry it out in a proper manner.

There is also something special about sitting around a simple fire in a circle. We are all equal here in this circle. We are each important in this circle. A circle itself has great significance and cultural meaning to me. My Grandfather is part of that circle of Native Americans known as the Earth People, and the Peace People by their ancient contemporaries. The invaders from Europe called them Sioux. The ancient shelter they used, a tee-pee structure, at its base is a circle. Its central fire-place and most camp fires are built in a circle. The stone-people-lodge is built in a circle. Birds nest in a circle. The Earth mother is a circular sphere. My experience as a humble shaman reveals to me that we live our lives like circles without end, from one world to the next. 'In a circle', is defined literally as a ceremony in the Lakota language. The circle symbolizes the harmony and connectedness of all things which is knowledge paramount to your success on earth as a human inhabitant.

"How many of you have come here this evening looking for something to enhance your lives? (*Everyone seemed to nod or raise their hands.*) Do you have an awareness regarding the power of a stone-people-lodge ceremony? (*Almost everyone nodded.*) I will regard you each as spiritual explorers, since you actually made it here to this moment in time beyond your fast moving schedules. Some of you had to overcome your personal fears. I assure you that only health and help has ever come to those that participate with me in this manner. Some of you had to overcome physical challenges. I commend you and want you to know this is not an endurance test. I had a man recently come to one of my stone-people-lodge ceremonies who, when it came time to enter, removed his prosthetic legs and one prosthetic arm. I am still inspired by his courage and he told me afterwards what a special experience it had been to talk to Spirit in this way. Many of you have embarked on a quest to find and experience the sacred in your lives. I consider what we are going to accomplish together tonight an example of the sacred. (*I viewed blank stares on the faces of the participants.*) Sacred is where a person's search for truth and an understanding of a higher power beyond yourself has led you. I believe we are each connected by the divine intelligence of our universe and that we carry this special light from lifetime to lifetime. Perhaps you will be touched by the sacred this evening in what my Grandfather Black Elk referred to as this *tunkan tipi*? *Tun* means 'birth', and *kan* means 'age', *tipi* means 'house', and together they refer to a rebirthing experience."

"We have several physicists taking part in our ceremony tonight. (I make eye contact with each of them). I admire the work that you do to help us understand our world. In my conversations with several of you, we discussed how the sacred aspects of our stone-people-lodge and physics are becoming part of the same discussion. We will be looking into the real physics of Mother Earth tonight. She knows, smells, tastes, sees, and hears everything. We will poke a little hole in the center of her ground that we will be praying on. This will allow her to breathe and communicate to us. We will put these hot stones in that center and offer them a little sage, a little sweet grass, a little cedar, and a little water, and we will honor her in this manner. This is one of man's oldest and direct forms of communicating with nature, in search of that individual wisdom that underlies each of our beings. The center of that circle will be our center. Its circumference will stretch into infinite space".

"I suspect that most of you have all been touched by the sacred at some point in your lives. You may also remember a moment of feeling especially connected to the Earth Mother. Others of you may remember a time when the veils of the mundane were lifted from your consciousness for you to perceive something extraordinary. Some of you have had the feeling of closeness to the sacred in the beauty of the natural world. Some of you have experienced the sacred by being inspired by another's words or song. Some of you may have experienced the sacred at a religious service. We will consciously focus our thoughts this evening in this stone-people-lodge ceremony. We are each quite powerful. In this ceremony we will connect our thoughts with Great Spirit to activate our intention through this sacred implement. (*I show them my Sacred Pipe.*) I will put these two pieces together, this stick and this stone, representing male and female. I will ask for help from the powers of the four directions, and sky father, and earth mother, and the eagle and hawk nations. For many of you, Spirit and mind will merge. The powers of Great Spirit through the powers of the four directions can be activated by your good words and thoughts. We will utilize a simple smoking mixture made up of the bark of our red osier dogwood, mixed with several herbs and a little natural tobacco. Not the kind with chemical additives. You will have an opportunity to connect your thoughts to the creative purpose through this action. You will also have an opportunity to speak in harmony with the highest principle to help manifest your requests. When you see that it already exists, then your declaration is complete and you can say thank you to all of the energies of the universe that helped create it".

"A sacred man or woman walks in that overlap of these dimensions when they accomplish this work. Those of you that work in the field of physics know that if you are able to picture two spheres merging, the section where they overlap is called a vesica pisces. If one sphere represents the supernatural and the other our natural reality, the phenomenon that you may experience within this stone-people-lodge can often be understood in the pure potential symbolized within their overlap-a vesica pisces".

"As children by our parents, and later as young adults by our teachers, we are taught what is real and what is not. In a similar vein it was Einstein who said, 'It is the theory that tells us what to look for in an experiment. Without a theory most data would fly by unnoticed.' Most people have experienced some sacred moment of the overlapping and creation of the vesica pisces in their lives, but simply fail to notice. This is why I have always felt a stone-people-lodge can be a life changing experience, because it often brings into focus the overlapping, creating, seeing, and even clear understanding of data you might have missed under ordinary circumstances."

The moonlight poured into our lodge as if a tidal wave had occurred the moment I opened the blanketed flap after the first segment of our ceremony. The freshness of the night air worked its magic on each of us, as we were reborn each segment of our intense four door ritual. Many people spoke to me after regarding what they learned and what blessings they received. Many saw the floating balls of light from the spirit realm that usually appeared in my ceremonies during the healing segment of the lodge. Others heard and some saw the colored shapes of light that appeared within that infinite space.

The following is what one physicist had to say to me after our stone-people-lodge ceremony: "The roots of modern day physics can be found in thoughts from the Greeks who inquired into the essential nature of all things. They developed tools to look into the fundamental building blocks of matter and were surprised when they found that part of that composition included empty space. At this quantum level they discovered that their attempts to measure this phenomenon actually affected it. This led them to realize that consciousness has to be integrated into our understanding of matter. The perceiving subject could no longer be separated from the object under observation. They discovered that time, space, and consciousness, are intimately interrelated and inseparable. They realized that a higher dimension must exist outside our perceptions of time in which everything is interconnected. They found out there is no such thing as an observer, we are all participants. They ended up describing quantum objects as neither wave nor particle. 'They do not exist; yet do not-not exist'. Telepathy, clairvoyance, precognition, remote viewing, and many other phenomena were called into question for many years until scientific experiments now measure and document them. The worlds that you and I work in, Red Hawk, are definitely converging."

QUESTION 67

Q You have mentioned "wisdom holders" in our ceremonies from time to time and I was hoping you might be able to shed further light on them for me this evening?

TJL Wisdom holders are human beings who have been initiated into the mysteries of Nature by the "universal mind" of Great Spirit. This wisdom is often passed along to those entities by celestial beings chosen for the task based on their appropriate levels of advancement.

QUESTION 68

Q You mentioned this evening that deer were spiritual allies of yours. You also shared with us that help from the "animal nations" was often overlooked by those on other sacred pathways of attainment. Is there anything further you can share about your deep connection with deer, and does that indicate that you carry what your Grandfather referred to as "deer medicine"?

TJL My first recollection this lifetime of having an affinity for deer came on a sultry evening in the Central Valley of California while watching Walt

Disney's Bambi in living color with my Dad, Mom, and two sisters at our local drive-in theatre. Our family had recently moved into a modern 1950's style rambler in a small Central California farm community where no actual deer contact could have been made. I must have been around five years of age when I viewed that movie and fell in love with those cute gangly furry creatures.

During my years managing parks, especially at Wilderness Gardens Preserve, members of the deer nation crossed my path during my time in their wild backcountry on numerous occasions. I had no idea why we felt so comfortable together but I always enjoyed the serene aspect of our moments there. That peaceful energy that existed between us seemed to grow stronger over our years of interface. After I agreed to carry a sacred pipe through Grandfather and Red Buffalo the deer nation became one of the beings along with the elk nation that I received help from each time I filled my pipe. Deer have been a part of many sacred activities I have participated in through my humble shaman altar.

One of the most powerful and unique deer moments I have ever experienced came with one of my shaman teachers, Red Buffalo, near his home on the Yankton Reservation in Eastern South Dakota. After completing a stone-people-lodge ceremony the evening before to ask Great Spirit for help with the approaching Sun Dance, including a request for a deer to be utilized for the feast after the dance, we positioned ourselves in a sage scrub environment near the Missouri River. On that occasion after several hours of patient viewing I witnessed a buck walk slowly forward out of the shadows to peer directly at us in anticipation of Steve's shot. He moved slowly and seemed to intentionally turn to present himself. His glistening black eyes seemed to peer directly into my soul. In that moment when Red Buffalo's shot rang out another sacred side to my relationship with the deer nation was revealed. We honored him with a sacred song, a smudging of sage and sweet grass, and prayers of thanks to Great Spirit for the food we would have to share after the Sun Dance. Great Spirit had revealed to me how powerful the deer connection was to our altar.

Now days I enjoy my solitude like many of the deer that pass through our property on the point next to the Puget Sound that we were directed to by my angel so many years ago. Like a deer I have a tendency to check people out from my sacred forest before I reveal myself to them. The deer out here often times sleep overnight next to my art studio and I know they feel the power of our connection there. I still enjoy watching their movements after many years of doing so, and especially enjoy the bambi-like babies that grow into young adults right before our eyes.

Another recent deer connection occurred on an overnight excursion to a rugged slope above

East Sound on Orcas Island in the San Juan Islands. I was looking forward to a few hours of star watching and special meditation time with my sacred pipe and small drum after doing some stone-people- lodge work the night before at the time. As I worked my way up the slope from where I had parked my pick-up I found a deer trail that switched-back and forth making my access relatively easy through the tangle of stone and scrub that I was walking through. After moving steadily towards my intended camping sight for about an hour I arrived at the clearing that I had held in my mind's eye. It was a glorious sight on a ledge overlooking splashes of rainbow color and reflections of starlight floating on the sea with a 180 degree view of the islands and sea. When dawn broke after I awoke I began to drum an honoring song followed by my pipe filling song. I then began to fill, pray, and smoke my sacred pipe. I was soon startled when I felt something nudging my right shoulder. It was in that moment that I realized a young doe had sauntered up beside me without my detecting her presence. I had never been approached in that stealthy a manor before by a deer in the wild. She appeared to be quite typical, honey colored thick coat, deep glistening black eyes and nose, with black tail standing quite still now before me. She nudged me again as if to say I now need your attention. When she turned slowly before me the other side of her body revealed her fur was matted with blood and I saw an open wound. I surmised by the size of the wound she had taken a glancing blow from a car down on the road and had apparently come up the trail for shelter and possible survival away from human beings. As she approached my sacred pipe laying now on the sage before me I realized what she had come after. The natural tobacco sitting on my makeshift altar seemed to be her intended medicinal target. After shaking out all that I had onto a flat rock she gobbled up every last grain as if I had prescribed to her the medicine that would help with her healing. As she sauntered down the trail and disappeared around a rock outcropping I felt once again the kindred spiritual side of what became a powerful literal aspect to the "deer medicine" that I have carried for many years.

QUESTION 69

Q Could you explain the giant head statuary of Easter Island?

TJL The gigantic heads are relics from the primeval giants of the fourth manifestation of human beings on Atlantis. Most of these mighty sorcerers represented by the heads disappeared under the seas after the sinking caused by an axial disturbance. Easter Island was part of that lost continent.

QUESTION 70

Q Would you mind clarifying what exactly humble shaman consciousness is?

TJL I believe we are each capable of learning from our living. We and the world are not two separate entities. We are the world and we can transform the world in which we live by transforming our relationship to it. A wise man once said we must be twice born, the first from our mother's womb and the second to our higher consciousness. Human beings have waged wars against the earth and each other for so long we have forgotten that our relationship to our planet has a direct correlation to our own well-being. It is time for the human race to grow up and treat our real mother the Earth with respect and love. True peace on Earth will follow.

The sanity and wisdom of many of the ancient indigenous peoples of our Earth Mother still hold that awareness. It is said that when our cumulative consciousness reaches a tipping point regarding an appropriate relationship to the Earth Mother then harmony and peace will come naturally to all beings.

Like many who have walked a similar path before me, I have come to recognize that humanity has only touched the surface of its vast potential. Modern physics now explains that our thoughts at certain moments have the ability to affect and change physical mass. Focused thoughts are capable of interacting with matter at the sub-atomic level. The ancients knew this to be a very real mechanism of what they called cosmic consciousness. If particles of matter come into and out of existence based solely on intention, unlimited consciousness can turn the possibility of something, into something real. This form of "humble shaman consciousness" continues to elude the majority of contemporary minds. That sharing of the quantum physics that a shaman is familiar with in ceremony has been one of the most important aspects of my exploration. A ripple in the water is capable of forming many rings. I want to be perfectly clear that you do not need to be a shaman to attain higher consciousness just as you do not need to be an electrician to turn on a light. Can we transcend our current understanding of the world in which we live? Will we be witness to a transformation of the collective mind by simply helping people to understand on an individual basis?

Great minds have predicted that man possesses the potential to accomplish almost anything. Our hearts want to believe this but our intellects so far have not allowed it. We must connect our hearts to our minds. Einstein felt that behind the secrets of nature something "subtle and inexplicable exists". The more we know today the greater our ability to expand our knowledge about it.

Many indigenous ceremonies and rituals are designed to awaken mankind. They are about honor, integrity, and service to others. They are about piercing the veil between man and Great Spirit. Perhaps one day humanity will take a leap of faith to understand that we have the ability, knowledge, and wealth to educate and take care of everyone. The growing contrast between the elite privileged beings and the impoverished ones could end in an instant of caring. No orphans need be left behind. If we each affect a basic transformation of self, the whole consciousness of the world in which we live would shift. We must discard aggression, ruthless ambition, greed, hatred, envy, and jealousy to bring about a new collective mind and heart.

One of the oldest written documents on the planet from the Upanishads, the "Rig Veda", states that, "Without effort one world will pass into another". Maybe that ancient author got it right back then. Might that document refer to a cosmic passage into a higher consciousness, to a new wave length that ancient prophecies speak about as the real heaven here on Earth? I am still hopeful a new and prosperous harmonic chapter in our human story may yet unfold with love and compassion as its primary focus. Act selflessly and cultivate a spirit of service toward all beings. This may be the ultimate reality necessary to bring about our next "Great Age" where the greatest power may simply be the kindness in your heart.

QUESTION 71

Q Have you ever heard of "The Doctrine of Spirit", and if so what exactly is it?

TJL The "Doctrine of Spirit" is an ancient concept that teaches that in every kingdom of nature, all life is animated by God, or what I refer to as Great Spirit.

QUESTION 72

Q What happens at the beginning of every new Earth incarnation?

TJL My angel states that at the beginning of every new Earth, referenced in my books, just as human beings receive a new body passing into a new womb and new life, so too does our planet receive a more perfect covering to begin its next world from the matrix of space as it moves once again into objectivity.

QUESTION 73

Q Could you help me understand what you mean when you speak about prana?

.

TJL Prana is the essence of life and the vital force which animates matter. The earliest recorded history recognizing this energy appears in China where it was known as ch'i. It is referred to as prana in Indian yogic texts. In Japan it was known as k'i. This life force sustains us here on Earth and is considered universal energy. Though it is in all forms of matter it is not matter itself. I utilize it in several aspects of the sacred work that I am involved with.

It has relieved pain in some of those that I have helped. It can be projected at a distance. It can be accumulated through the air you breathe, the food you eat, or the liquid you consume. Within a stone-people-lodge, I was able to see an indication of who people are as their prana fields glow in that environment. All living organisms exchange this energy with the universe. When the flow of this energy is restricted or becomes imbalanced then the organism becomes sick. If the flow ceases altogether, then so does that individual life.

QUESTION 74

Q How has your work as a humble shaman influenced your work as an artist?

TJL I am certain I have enhanced my focus and attention to detail in my practice of each endeavor. I receive great joy from each process and know I have expanded my consciousness in many ways. I firmly believe that pure color holds many keys to understanding our universe. Color is a spiritual language in and of itself. If you examine the language of light and color, you will eventually understand your own connection to the Divine more clearly. At the center of each activity is a chance to help people see beyond mundane appearances so they might someday fully understand who they are and why they are here.

QUESTION 75

Q What else can you tell us about the "Prophecy of the Seven Cradles of Civilization?

TJL The prophecy predicts that there will be seven major land masses involved in the seven primary manifestations of humanity during this incarnation of planet Earth.

The first of these was known as the imperishable sacred land. This was the first solid ground utilized by the Divine Benefactors on which the first human beings came into being. It is said this sacred land mass will still be intact to the end of all seven worlds of the seventh incarnation of Earth.

The second of these land masses was known as the Hyperborean Land. It was also referred to as the North Polar continent. It was a land that had no winter and continuous day light. It is said the Divine Benefactors created the second manifestation of human beings there. It existed southward and westward from what we call the North Pole, including Northern Asia.

The third of these land masses was known as Lemuria. It is said the Divine Benefactors incarnated into the third manifestation of humankind within this land in order to endow us with intellect. Ceylon and Sumatra, parts of Africa, to the Indian Ocean and Australia, Tasmania, to the Anarctic Circle, stretching to parts of the Pacific Ocean including California. While this gigantic land mass existed above the seas there was no

North or South American land masses, and hardly any African, European, and Asian areas.

The fourth of these land masses was made of seven great islands and was known as Atlantis. It is said they existed from the eastern coast of North America and South America to parts of the west coast of Africa, to Greenland and the Azore islands. An axial disturbance caused most of the land mass to disappear under the seas leaving only the island that Plato described finally sinking many years later.

The Americas are the fifth land mass that was prophesied in our age.

The other two have yet to be identified and perhaps do not yet exist.

QUESTION 76

Q You have utilized the word manvantara from Hindu philosophy to describe each of the seven worlds that will take place within our present incarnation of Earth. Would you please review what is meant by manvantara?

TJL Manvantara's are simply defined as the active periods within our universe such as the active world we are currently a part of.

QUESTION 77

Q You have utilized the word pralaya from Hindu philosophy to describe periods of time between the worlds we have already experienced, and will experience in our future. Would you please review for me what is meant by pralaya.

TJL Pralaya's are simply defined as the restful periods between the worlds we have experienced and will experience in our future. A maha pralaya refers to the time at the end of seven manvantara's in which a major restful period occurs at the end of each of the predicted seven Earth incarnations.

QUESTION 78

Q You have utilized the word kalpa from Hindu philosophy within your "Sacred Earth" teaching this evening. Would you please review for me the meaning of kalpa?

TJL A Kalpa describes a period during which a physical world comes into being, is formed, and eventually destroyed. As an example one of the four worlds we have experienced to date would be referred to as a kalpa. A maha kalpa would describe all seven worlds that we will experience in this incarnation of our Earth. At the beginning of every kalpa the Earth goes through a rebirthing process.

QUESTION 79

Q You have informed us that between world's major geological convulsions have taken place in our past, and will most likely take place in Earth's future. Could you shed any further light on this process?

TJL This process is known as "obscuration" and is usually viewed as the labor pains of the rebirth of the planet into the next world. These seven geo-logical changes correspond to the evolution of each of the seven worlds that we will experience during this the fourth incarnation of Earth.

QUESTION 80

Q You have described past worlds in your writing and your teaching within our ceremonies indicating major geological upheavals have occurred at the end of each world cycle. Is there anything you can share with us about the four incarnations of planet Earth that are each divided by seven worlds?

TJL We are currently taking part in the fourth world of the fourth incarnation of planet Earth.

The first incarnation of Earth, is described by fire, volcanoes, radiance, and no solidity. The second incarnation of Earth she described by luminous, dense, heavy air. The third incarnation of Earth is described by watery environments. The fourth incarnation of Earth is described as a gaseous fluid environment in transformation. Earth's surface has grown solid in order to be suitable for the establishment of human beings on its surface according to Great Spirit's plan for us.

QUESTION 81

Q In your first book your angel speaks to you about "the sacred peace" you will gain when you discover the place in the northern lands she sees for you and your family. What can you share with us here tonight about that sacred peace that you found?

TJL The sacred peace of the awakened soul evolves over many lifetimes and eventually comes to those who are conscious of the real spiritual existence that I have shared with you in my writing, teaching, and art. That peace of a mature soul grows sweeter over the years and is usually part of a pathway influenced by the higher powers.

QUESTION 82

Q Could you explain "the Way of the Tao"?

TJL "The Way of the Tao" is Chinese in origin, and literally translated as "the way of nature" in which all things come into being out of Darkness into Light, then pass out of Light back into Darkness, back and forth throughout time. Light and Dark were considered identical, only separated by our human minds. Neither principle is thought to be better than the other. Neither principle is thought to be stronger than the other. The secret of the

Tao then is to understand no matter what comes your way it is neither good nor bad, it simply is part of your way.

QUESTION 83

Q Would you explain the "Sufi Way" to me ?

TJL Certainly, Sufism is the philosophical free thinking of mysticism united with an entirely original symbolic and sensuous poetry. It grew and blossomed in the early centuries of the second millennium of the Christian era combining sensuousness and religious ecstasy in perfect harmony. The primary concept is a loving union of the soul with Great Spirit, on Earth nothing expressed that better than the love between man and woman.

QUESTION 84

Q Would you share what you know about the mythical Akashic Records?

TJL The Akashic Records are a body of knowledge that contains everything that every soul has ever thought, said, or done over the course of its existence as well as its future possibilities. In the process of opening these records a person must transition from a state of ordinary consciousness to a state of universal consciousness in which you recognize your absolute oneness with Great Spirit.

This state allows you to perceive the impressions and vibrations at a manageable rate which allows you to integrate them into your human experience. Akasha is a Sanskrit word describing the primary substance out of which all things are formed. It is comprised of such fineness that even the slightest vibration affects it. This energy can be described as a quality of light that our thoughts and emotions register upon. Therefore the records hold the archive of each soul as it has existed from lifetime to lifetime as different human beings. They are the catalogue of our experiences as an individual as we grow into our divine nature.

QUESTION 85

Q I have heard the term "fallen angels" mentioned by others apparently denigrating a segment of the angel population for some reason. Could you please clarify this matter for me?

TJL The archangels who helped create human beings on our planet and other helping angels "fell into matter" and sacrificed themselves to generation and the cycle of reincarnation so inner man could be developed. These angels gave up their natural status exchanging their impersonal individualities for individual personalities. They sacrificed their bliss for terrestrial lives, thus the term fallen into our material realm.

QUESTION 86

Q When will the next pralaya occur on Earth?

TJL The next pralaya will happen 16,000 years from now according to my angel.

QUESTION 87

Q What does the word creation mean to you?

TJL Creation is the light which comes from love. From my view that light comes from the Fire of Life, Great Spirit. Human beings and our entire world are constantly being purified by this source and all forms of the human spirit and genius continue ever upward through our evolving souls.

QUESTION 88

Q Could you talk about the dialogue you have shared with your angel over the years?

TJL Out of the silence usually before, during, or after a ceremony her voice entered my field of consciousness to help someone in some manner. Sometimes the person being helped was contacted directly by her and they also heard her voice speaking to them. During my initiation in the Great Pyramid she appeared in a physical form that was transparent yet had substance as I described in my first book. She explains she comes from a plane of consciousness different from our own, and that the song she gave me was intended to help me dial in to her frequency to hear her words more clearly throughout our years of working together in ceremony. It also solidified my knowing that we had physically met within that sacred temple.